WRITER'S INTERNET SOURCEBOOK

Writer's Internet Sourcebook

MICHAEL LEVIN

NO STARCH PRESS

SAN FRANCISCO

Printed in the United States of America
1 2 3 4 5 6 7 8 9 10—00 99 98 97

Trademarks
Trademarked names are used throughout this book. Rather than use a trademark symbol with every occurrence of a trademarked name, we are using the names only in an editorial fashion and to the benefit of the trademark owner, with no intention of infringement of the trademark.

Publisher: William Pollock
Project Editor: Karol Jurado
Cover Design and Composition: Derek Yee
Interior Design: Margery Cantor
Copyeditor: Carol Lombardi
Proofreader: Linda Medoff
Indexer: Matthew Spence

Distributed to the book trade in the United States and Canada by Publishers Group West, 4065 Hollis, P.O. Box 8843, Emeryville, California 94662, phone: 800-788-3123 or 510-548-4393, fax: 510-658-1834.

For information on translations or book distributors outside the United States, please contact No Starch Press directly:
No Starch Press
401 China Basin Street, Suite 108, San Francisco, CA 94107-2192
phone: 415-284-9900; fax: 415-284-9955; info@nostarch.com; www.nostarch.com

Library of Congress Cataloging-in-Publication Data
Levin, Michael Graubart.
Writer's Internet sourcebook / Michael Levin.
p. cm.
Includes index.
ISBN 1-886411-11-5 (pbk. : alk. paper)
1. Computer network resources—Directories. 2. Authorship-
-Computer network resources—Directories.
ZA4201.L48 1997
025.04—dc21 97-8055
CIP

For William Pollock, my Latin brother

TABLE OF CONTENTS

ACKNOWLEDGMENTS

My thanks first and foremost to Bill Pollock, my editor, publisher, and friend, whose idea this book is. I appreciate Bill's faith in my writing ability and his patience with my technical ability. The fact that a person with as limited a knack for new technology like me can write a book like this shows that the Internet truly is for everyone.

I'd like to thank next the people who gave freely of their time and expertise to create the hundreds of websites and Gopher menus reviewed in this book. The soul of the Internet is the idea of a free flow of information and ideas. Few "content providers" (the folks who actually write the information that you can read, download, print, and e-mail for free) make any money from their work. The website and Gopher menu authors share their knowledge with us out of a universal need to connect, to share, to build together. I thank them for what they have given the rest of us.

The staff of No Starch Press is an extraordinarily hard-working and friendly lot and any author would be extremely lucky to work with them. I certainly feel that way. My thanks to Carol Lombardi, the copy editor who made me sound a lot more knowledgeable than I really am. This beautiful volume was designed by Margery Cantor, who obviously has great reasons for taking pride in her work. Project Editor Karol Jurado, that early riser, is always cool, calm, and collected in the face of my endless questions and concerns. And thanks to Derek Yee for designing the fine cover that wraps this book and for composing its pages.

My special thanks to my fantastic team of interns, Anthony Tarzia, Charlotte Chen, and Corey Nickerson, who spent countless hours finding sites, checking references, and doing a million other things.

I predict great careers in writing for Charlotte and Corey and a great future in the film industry for Anthony.

If you have comments or suggestions about this book, or if you've got a site you'd like to see us review in the next edition, you can e-mail me at levin@nostarch.com. I'm looking forward to hearing from you.

Michael Levin

WHY YOU NEED THIS BOOK

Authors, Agents, and Publishers

Writing, by nature, is a lonely enterprise. Or at least it was until the Internet came along. Now it's possible to make contact in a microsecond with thousands of authors, agents, and publishers. You can find the names and e-mail addresses of a vast number of individuals whose ideas, business connections, and careers can help yours. And vice versa.

The toughest thing for a writer starting out is simply *to be heard*. We send manuscripts, queries, and requests for representation out into what feels like a great void. We wonder if anyone's paying attention, or if anyone ever will.

And it's never easy to *find the right person*, whether that person is a literary agent, an editor, a source of information, or a fellow author. Well, good news: finding the right people has just gotten a million times easier. This section of the book will help you make contact with the people you've been trying, successfully or otherwise, to track down by other, less organized means.

I was never much for buzzwords like "virtual community" until I started visiting the sites in this section of the book. Simply by visiting these sites, you can find the people you need for your writing career, and you can contact them via e-mail, which offers a sense of immediacy, egalitarianism, and ease that no other form of communication can provide.

Immediacy. There's something about the words "You Have Mail." Who's trying to contact us? What's it about? Could it be something important? I better check, and I better do it now. That's the sense of immediacy and urgency that you get when you write to someone, even someone you've never met, via e-mail. You get access to people who otherwise might be very difficult to reach. You get to say everything you want to say, without fear of interruption. And when you send someone an e-mail, you have that person's full attention, at least for the time it takes to read your message.

Egalitarianism. The most powerful CEO and the lowliest teenage hacker each receive exactly the same amount of space on an Incoming Mail docket: one line. All e-mails, you might say, are created equal. There's no fancy letterhead to make one letter seem more important than another. All it takes is an e-mail address of your own, which now costs between twelve and twenty dollars a month, and you are a player. Your words have to be taken seriously.

Ease. To reply to an e-mail letter takes a couple of keystrokes or clicks of the mouse. No stamps, no envelopes, no printers, no telephone answering machines, no "telephone tag," no long distance charges. E-mail makes it extremely easy for someone to respond to you.

Put these three benefits together—immediacy, egalitarianism, and ease—and suddenly your computer becomes an unparalleled tool for finding, contacting, and most important, *getting heard* by the people you need to take your writing career to the next level.

Study these sites carefully. Find the people you need, and get to know them.

Books

In the early 1980s, Isaac Asimov was asked whether computers could ever completely replace books. His answer, perhaps not unsurprisingly, was yes. He predicted that computers would eventually become small and portable (he got that one right) and that they would also take on a softer, more aesthetic feel. At some point, he said, people will start designing computers not like hard metallic objects but instead like soft, comfortable, appealing things—like books.

Well, we haven't quite reached that stage yet. The Internet hasn't quite obsolesced the printed book. Could it happen? Only when a computer matches the Asimovian dream of something you can curl up with, under an apple tree or in bed. In the meantime, the Internet makes it easier to buy books, to learn about books, to find out which books have won awards, and to discover which books are worth your time.

Looking to buy a book? This section offers you reviews of the best online booksellers, including the enormous Amazon.com, the chains, and many smaller specialty and antiquarian bookstores in the U.S. and the U.K. that will find a specific book for you, no matter how old or how rare.

Looking to find out something good to read? Check out the lists of award-winning books in all genres and visit a goodly number of sites that offer reviews of new works.

Looking to sell rights for your work but can't fly to Frankfurt for the book fair there? International book fairs are opportunities for publishers, authors, buyers of foreign and translation rights to meet and mingle and find out what's new. The average author usually cannot afford to travel to book fairs, but in this section of the *Writer's Internet Sourcebook*, you'll learn how to have your works represented at book fairs around the world.

Computers and the Internet haven't replaced the printed word, but they've made the printed word a lot easier to find. Find out how, here.

Genres

Inherent in our nature is the need to connect with others like ourselves. This ancient human desire finds full expression on the Internet, where writers of every stripe find each other and create communities, niches, and virtual worlds where they can share their ideas, their writing, and sometimes their software.

If you're already committed to a particular genre, be it young adult writing, screenwriting, or mysteries, or whatever, you certainly don't need me to suggest to you to visit the sites I've culled from the vast number of Internet sites available in your field. I would like to suggest strongly that you read through this entire section quite carefully and that you visit as many of these sites as you can.

Taken together, the sites in each of these sections is the equivalent of one or more cutting-edge seminars on that field or genre of writing. For the investment of your time—none of these sites requires any money—you can become an expert in a field of writing that you might never have thought much about. You can develop a second specialty or expertise in addition to the kind of writing you do now. You can find a new set of markets for your work, increasing your income, your visibility, your audience, and your sense of satisfaction with writing.

Never thought of writing for teenagers? Or for the movies? Never considered spinning a romance or a mystery to pay the bills while you're working on the Great American (or Great Canadian, or Great New Zealand) Novel? You can learn how, here, quickly, and easily. Think of it as cross-training for writers. Enjoy yourself.

A word about the Journalism sites: no matter what your field, be sure to examine these sites. You'll be amazed at how much information, how many contacts, how many sources are yours for the asking.

Improving Your Writing

A good writer is a writer who wants to improve. We can always broaden our knowledge of grammar and usage and we can always become better writers. How, you ask? The Internet offers dozens of sites dedicated to the rules of grammar. I've chosen the best of those sites and am happy to present them here. Copy editors, those wonderful people who make your writing look better, neater, and more grammatically precise than you can, may also choose from a superlative variety of sites focused on their craft. And you can find a number of writing classes available via the Web.

How Writers Make Money Online

This section shows you the money. Here you'll find permanent and project-oriented jobs for writers of all kinds. You'll learn how to promote and market your book on and off the Internet. You'll discover all the best places on the Web for publishing your work online—on your own website, or in a Zine. You can even learn to start a Zine of your own.

Reference Resources on the Internet

This might just be my favorite section of this book, because it turns your computer into an astonishingly powerful reference tool. The urge to organize practically all human knowledge is satisfied here. Whatever your question, a brief trip into the sites listed below will find you the answer you want . . . and provoke even more questions. A most enjoyable ride awaits you. The only difficult thing will be to pull yourself away from these fantastic websites and get back to your writing.

WHAT DO YOU DO IF YOU CAN'T FIND A PARTICULAR SITE?

When the Rolling Stones sang "You Can't Always Get What You Want," they might have had the Internet in mind. There you are, gearing up to find a particular reference, text, or quotation, ready to type in the world's longest URL, and everything goes wrong: The link doesn't work, the file is not found, the site doesn't exist, or you're informed that your software has "performed an illegal operation and will be shut down." Harrumph.

Internet sites disappear because they exist strictly at the whim of the person (or group) who posts them. Anyone can launch a website and just as quickly take it down—or stop paying the host of their website and have their account canceled. And sites move as their hosts move their accounts, which means that the site may be on the Internet but not at the address where we last visited it. And they don't necessarily leave a forwarding address.

Web browsers have their problems too. For example, America Online's own Web browser appears to have some limitations. When I used it I found that it wouldn't connect to hundreds of sites. It claimed that sites didn't exist when I knew they did because I had just visited them on another machine using Netscape Navigator and a direct connection to an Internet Service Provider.

The solution? If you're using America Online version 3.0 or higher, follow their instructions for downloading, installing, and using Netscape Navigator with America Online. Or, sign up with an ISP and run either Netscape Navigator or Microsoft's Internet Explorer through them. Making the switch may solve many of your Web browsing problems.

I Still Can't Find That Site

What do you do if you can't find a site we recommend, or one to which you've been directed by a site listed here in this book? Before you despair, work your way back through the site's address by lopping off everything after the first backslash to shorten the URL. Then try connecting to that site.

Those slashes (/) between the words in a site's address represent different levels of information (like directories and sub-directories in DOS/Windows or Folders in the Macintosh world). What often happens is that while the main site is still there, a particular piece of it has been renamed or been deleted entirely. Working your way back up to the top level of the site will often bring you to its *home page*, from which you can begin searching for the particular missing piece.

For example, if you can't find

http://www.freckles.com/~gigglepuss/chachacha.htm

try the first part

http://www.freckles.com/~gigglepuss

to see if **~gigglepuss** (possibly someone who rents space from **freckles.com**) still exists. If no joy here, try **http://www.freckles.com** to see if you can find out anything about either **chachacha.htm** or **~gigglepuss**.

If this strategy doesn't work and you know the name of the site that you're trying to reach, try searching for it by name to see if it's still around but maybe in a different place. Here are the search engines that we recommend with a couple of tips for using each:

AltaVista (http://www.altavista.digital.com) is the search engine we like best. When you reach it, type the name of the site you're searching for or words that describe it into the box on your screen and press the SUBMIT button. To limit the number of sites that it finds to only those containing exactly the words that you type in, enclose your search words in quotation marks: "chocolate ice cream" will get you far fewer—and probably far more useful—matches than chocolate ice cream. (About 100,000 or more without quotes; 900 or so with quotes.) You can also search Usenet newsgroups with AltaVista by clicking the SEARCH box up top and choosing "Usenet" instead of "the Web" and then performing your search. Search these for mentions of the site you want to find—other people may be looking for it too.

Yahoo! (http://www.yahoo.com) is another very popular search tool. When using it you can select a category link from your screen (like "Arts and Humanities"), and drill down through it to find the topic you're interested in. Or, type your search words into the box and press **SEARCH**. A search for "chocolate ice cream" in Yahoo! turned up only about six sites when I last checked; many fewer than with AltaVista.

Excite (http://www.excite.com) is still another alternative. Search it the same way that you would AltaVista—enclose your search words in quotation marks for best results.

Deja News will search the universe of Usenet newsgroups (http://www.dejanews.com/). This astonishing search engine will examine the messages in newsgroups throughout the world to find those that most nearly match your query. Follow the links to messages that seem relevant and then follow the threads of conversations to look for suggestions of interesting websites. (As with AltaVista and Excite, enclose your query in quotation marks for best results.)

The Internet rewards the patient user. Remember that it's still in its infancy and that you'll get more adept with time. Have fun, learn, create . . . and let us know what you find.

CHAPTER ONE

AGENTS

The two questions most commonly asked by new authors are (1) How do I protect my work from theft? and (2) How do I find an agent? For protecting your work, see Chapter 9, "Copyright." For finding an agent, here are four traditional ways:

1. Find a copy of *Literary Marketplace* in the reference section of your public library. Locate the section on Literary Agents. Do a mass mailing to all those agents who accept unsolicited manuscripts in your genre of work. In your cover letter, explain briefly who you are and what your book is. Include a chapter-by-chapter breakdown and two or three sample chapters (the first chapters if it's fiction). Wait and see who's interested.

2. Attend writers' conferences, many of which are listed in Chapter 5, "Writers' Conferences and Groups." Walk up to an agent (who will not bite) and say, "I'm almost done with my (novel/nonfiction book proposal/whatever). Could I please have your business card?" The agent will hand you a card with a warm smile. When you send the same package as in Step 1 above, mention in the first paragraph that you met them at the Oshkosh Writers' Festival.

3. Look in the preface of your favorite books to see whether the author acknowledged his or her agent. This is more common in recently published books. Or go back to the reference section of

your public library and look up your favorite author in *Contemporary Authors*, a wonderful encyclopedia of English-speaking authors. Send the agent the same package as in Step 1, but this time with a first paragraph that begins with something like, "I understand that you represent Anne Author, who is one of my favorite writers. Perhaps we have some literary taste in common."

4. Lean on any published authors you've ever met and ask them to look at your work. The worst that can happen is they'll say no; the best is that they'll introduce you to their agent or publisher. This is by far the best way to make something happen, for several reasons. First, the agent or editor will respond promptly, as a favor to their author, and second, the agent or editor will give the manuscript an unusually careful reading—for the same reason.

You might also send your favorite authors a Step 1 package. You can write to them care of their agent (see Step 3 to find out who their agent is), care of their publisher (not always the most reliable or speedy way of getting in touch), or directly, if their street or e-mail address is available via one of the search engines listed in Appendix A: "Bookmark Essentials."

The newest way to find an agent is via the Internet. Check out the listings in this section; you'll be amazed at how easy it is to make contact with those elusive beings called literary agents.

You Too Can Be a Literary Agent

Did you know that you can become a literary agent right now? Today? You can! There's no licensing board, no test to pass, no probationary period. Just announce to the world that you're a literary agent, and writers with fragile dreams of publishing glory will send you manuscripts—and reading fees, too. That's right—you can charge reading fees even though you've never represented a single author, never sold a manuscript, never gotten anyone a deal of any kind. And you can use the Internet to solicit reading fees from would-be authors around the globe. This is the kind of sleazy operator that you as a writer should avoid.

I therefore urge all budding writers to never send a reading fee to any agency under any circumstances. The reputable agents I know never charge reading fees. Are there reputable agents who do charge reading fees? Perhaps. But for the most part, beware of chiselers and dishonest people who are simply trying to separate you from your money. Don't get taken. Don't send a nickel to any agent. Let them make *you* money—don't let them take yours!

Once more, with feeling: Anyone can post a Web page; anyone can claim to be an agent. Keep your checkbook in the drawer—especially when you're surfing the Web. Got it?

We've listed just a few sites in this section because you can find most Internet-savvy agents through the first site—The Internet Directory of Literary Agents.

Keep in mind: Most successful agents will still want to see your work in traditional, hard-copy form. Ironically, just because you're at technology's cutting edge doesn't mean the publishing industry has gotten there as well.

Also, be sure to read the eye-opening article "Literary Agents: The View from the Other Side" (page 4) as well as other material posted by the Writer's Guild of America.

The Internet Directory of Literary Agents

RECOMMENDED

http://www.writers.net/agents.html

Most impressive! This baby is loaded with dozens of agents: Click on their names to get street and e-mail addresses, phone numbers, descriptions of their agencies, and their fields of specialty. A great way to connect with agents while sparing yourself the usual time, aggravation, and expense of photocopies and mailings. My hat's off to the kind folks at Writers.Net for this invaluable service to the author in search of a literary agent. Bravo.

Another reason to praise this site is the fact that they banish any agents who charge reading fees.

"Literary Agents: The View from the Other Side"

RECOMMENDED

http://www.wga.org/journal/1996/0396/litagent.htm

Top literary agents comment on the agent–author relationship in this article from the Journal of the Writers Guild of America, West. If this article is no longer on the Net by the time you want to find it, by all means go to the WGA home page at *http://www.wga.org/index.html* and feast your eyes on all the other excellent articles and content that await you.

Studio B

http://www2.studiob.com/studiob/index.html

One of the leading literary agencies for computer book authors. They also provide complete book production services. Read about how the agency works; view their client list; find out how to get in contact with them. Other features: a news service offering writing tips, as well as interviews with authors and publishers; a mailing list through which you can get answers to your questions from industry experts; a "checklist" with hypertext links on the subject of how to write a bestseller; and a marketplace with classified ads from authors, publishers, and others.

Waterside Productions

http://www.waterside.com

Founded in 1982, Waterside Productions describes itself as the "premier computer book agency" and has negotiated over 5,000 contracts with more than 100 publishers. You can query the agency with your book idea; view their author/agent contract; learn how to publish your book electronically; read about the authors and publishers with whom they work; and get information about the annual computer book conference that Waterside produces.

CHAPTER TWO

AUTHORS AND AUTHOR DIRECTORIES

Just about every important author, living or otherwise, has a Web page. Some are the creations of publishing houses or public relations firms; their purpose is to connect readers with authors and sell books. If you have published books and don't have a Web page, you are depriving your fans and potential fans of the opportunity to get to know you better. Other Web pages are the products of fans or students. Some are simple homages to the authors; others provide extensive biographical and bibliographical detail.

The easiest way to find the Web pages of the author you're looking for is to search in the appropriate directory listed below. You'll also find links to other authors you might find interesting. In the second part of this section, we provide a few sample websites of authors, so you can know what to expect.

AUTHOR DIRECTORIES

Another Women Writers Links Page

http://we.got.net/docent/soquel/womwrt.htm

This modestly named website offers links to hundreds of women authors, poets, diarists and others, as well as to many titles, both well known and obscure. Click on a name and you'll get a brief biography, photographs, links to bookstores selling the writer's work, and more. I clicked on Anais Nin—whose diaries inspired generations of men and women to quit chasing middle-class respectability and move to Paris—and I found the bio, a link to the Nin Bookstore, information about her former home, and personal recollections by those who knew Anais Nin. If there's a woman author with a home page anywhere on the Web, chances are that you can find her here.

Of related interest: Women Writers' Resources

Authors' Pen: Authors Brief Biographies

http://www.books.com

Over 550 brief biographies and publishing histories of 20th-century authors, a "cafe" where you can meet authors who explain how to get published, and a reading group. You'll find a schedule for the various online meetings with authors. I was impressed with the caliber of comments in the reading group. This is worth your time.

Inkspot—Children's Writer and Illustrator Resource

http://www.interlog.com/~ohi/inkspot/

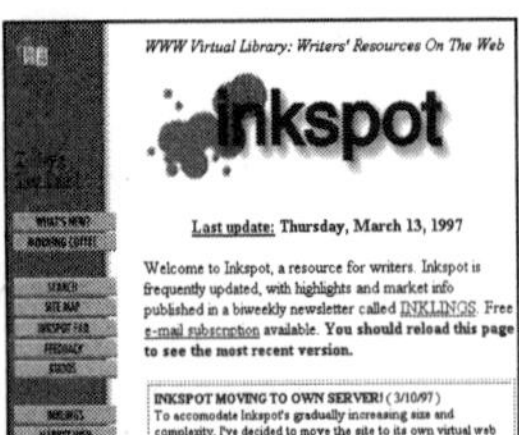

Here's an annotated directory of authors and illustrators with links to their websites. For instance, Margaret Atwood is best known for her adult novels, but she has also written several children's books; read about them at her homepage. The illustrators' list offers links to home pages of children's illustrators and also provides information about job opportunities.

Of related interest: Young Adult, Middle Grade, and Children's Writing

News about Publishing

http://www.canoe.ca/Jambooks/home.html

Jam!, a hip Canadian website, offers the latest news about authors from media outlets around the world. You'll find a list of Canadian bestsellers and reviews of many new books, as well as information about pop culture in all its manifestations. The publishing articles are varied and interesting: When I looked in, articles included an interview with author Ruth Rendell, a book taken off the shelves in anticipation of a libel action, an author calling a reviewer "asinine," and a sci fi author winning an award in France. An excellent way to keep up with the latest goings-on in the world of publishing.

Novelists, Inc.

http://www.ninc.com/

Founded in 1989, this group consists of 500 authors who have each published at least two works of popular fiction. Their website offers writing tools and tips (like a "self-editing checklist"), favorite research websites, links to authors' home pages, an application form for membership, and samples of articles from their newsletter. The articles look good—topics include "Contracts: Ten Things to Negotiate and What's Not Worth Your Time," "My First Time, or an Anecdotal History of An Author's First Time Hitting *The New York Times* Bestseller List," "The Art of the Tax Form: How the Internal Revenue Code Affects Novelists." That last piece, authored by a CPA and small business consultant, offers sophisticated advice on home office deductions, incorporation, estimated taxes, pension plans, and IRAs. Well worth your time.

Of related interest: Essays on Writing and Publishing

WritersNet Directory of Authors and Agents

http://www.writers.net

This site lists contact information for thousands of authors, including their e-mail addresses and, in many cases, their phone numbers and home addresses, along with their publication history and whether they are available for freelance writing. You can search by author name, browse the list, or search by any of approximately one hundred topics or genres. This address also includes a list of literary agents that is reviewed in Chapter 1, "Agents."

AUTHOR'S HOME PAGES

Beat Generation

http://www.charm.net/~brooklyn/litkicks.html

The Beat Generation get their due here with well-written hypertext biographies of Jack Kerouac, Allen Ginsberg, Neal Cassady, William S. Burroughs, Lawrence Ferlinghetti, and other '50s and '60s beat writers. Author Levi Asher pays homage to a generation of writers that continues to capture the imagination of young readers and writers. You'll find interviews, samples of the Beats' work, and the details of the time when the website's author auditioned for the film version of *On The Road*. Get out your bongos and drop in here.

F. Scott Fitzgerald Centenary Home Page

http://www.sc.edu/fitzgerald/index.html

The rich are different from you and me—they have faster microprocessors. That's what F. Scott Fitzgerald would say if he were here today. Think of the novels he'd write: *This Side of Pentium, Tender Is the Newsgroup, The Great Gopher.* Well, the good news is you don't have to think about those titles at all. Instead, visit this site and you'll find bibliographies of the works of and about Scott and Zelda, a brief life of Fitzgerald, a chronology of the lives of Scott and Zelda, essays and articles, Fitzgerald Facts, and Fitzgerald Quotations.

James Joyce

http:/www.mcs.net/~jorn/html/jj.html

Joyce would have loved the Internet and, for all I know, he invented it. The organization, or lack thereof, of cyberspace mirrors most nearly, of all authors, the mind of the author of *Finnegan's Wake.* A website worthy of Joyce, this one provides as-yet-unpublished research on Joyce's notebooks and early drafts, a biographical sketch, a condensed timeline, a chapter-by-chapter look at *Ulysses* and its riddles, news about the battle over the royalties on *Ulysses*, a chapter-by-chapter plot sketch of *Finnegans Wake* . . . and "exhaustive hypertext annotations of the puns and allusions in a single paragraph" of *Finnegans Wake*, which amounts to over 100Kb of text. For the insatiable, this site also includes links to ten or so other Joyce sites.

Franz Kafka

http://www.cowland.com/josephk/josephk.htm

The author of tender, lighthearted classics like *The Castle*, *The Trial*, *Amerika*, and *Metamorphosis* is now featured in a Web page so cunningly constructed that your browser can enter but never leave. Kafka fans, many of whom also belong to the Usenet discussion groups alt.depression, alt.misery, and alt.whybother, will feel at home here as they peruse a listing of Schocken's library of Kafka, a chronology of his life, a bibliography on Kafka, and links to sites with Kafka texts. Thank you, C.M. Wisniewski; pass the Prozac.

Danielle Steel

http://www.daniellesteel.com

The author of 38 published novels gives you a warm welcome along with a brief biography, a "screening room" listing her NBC television movies, a trivia contest, and a scrapbook. An attractive website for her millions of fans. Keywords: moist, throbbing.

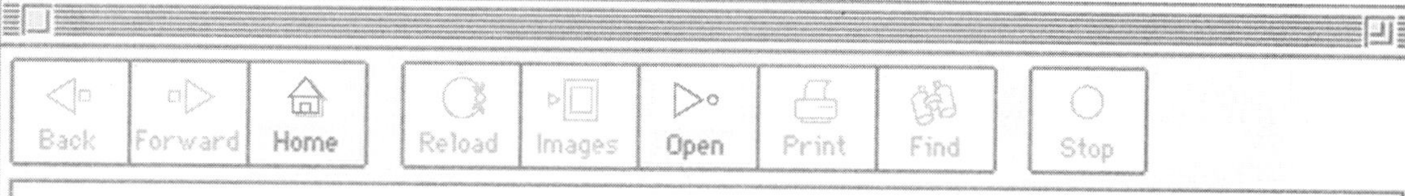

CHAPTER THREE

PROFESSIONAL ORGANIZATIONS

Here you will find 15 of America's leading writing organizations for writers of all stripes. The websites have been chosen for this book because they offer information, for free, to all writers, regardless of whether one is a member. Writing groups are your voice on Capitol Hill, in the White House, with publishers, and with employers. They deserve your full support. You may find, through these pages, a group that you'd like to join. If you would like to see your group listed in the next edition of this book, please e-mail us at *writers@nostarch.com*.

American Society of Journalists and Authors

http://www.asja.org/

This leading organization of nonfiction writers offers at its website useful articles on electronic rights and "e-wrongs"; the electronic rights clause in magazine and newspaper articles; contract tips for freelancers; and information on copyright registration. You can also learn about their criteria for membership and discover what benefits come to their members, who are active magazine, newspaper, and nonfiction writers.

American Booksellers Association

RECOMMENDED

http://www.bookweb.org

America's largest trade association for booksellers. Its gorgeous, highly professional, and wonderfully useful website offers writers at all levels a great education about the business of selling books. Profiles of bookstores; statistics; a guide to creating reading groups in bookstores; book and author events; essays about genres (True Crime at the time of my visit); information on upcoming book fairs and festivals; a searchable database of booksellers and home pages; book news; and, of course, information on the annual ABA convention, Book Expo, make this website a first stop and bookmark for anyone serious about publishing.

American Library Association

http://www.ala.org/index.html

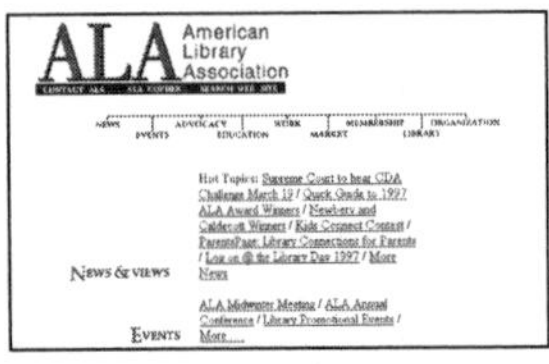

Job listings, information on banned books, news about libraries, and tons of information about how the publishing world and libraries intersect.

Association of American Publishers

http://www.publishers.org/

The principal trade organization of the publishing industry. You'll learn about copyright, "freedom to read," a compensation survey for authors, international freedom to publish, new technology, and much more. An information-rich website for those who wish to learn more about the publishing industry.

Bibliographical Society of America

http://aultgus.rutgers.edu/bsastuff/bsahome.html

A scholarly society for the textual and bibliographic study of books and manuscripts. Known primarily for their Tuesday night beer blasts, where scholars pound Budweiser and discuss in raucous tones the differences among analytic, textual, descriptive, and enumerative bibliography. Parental discretion advised. Just kidding. It's a serious site but I thought they'd get more hits if I talked about Budweiser.

Horror Writers Association

http://www.horror.org/hwa/

The darkest home page in cyberspace belongs to the Horror Writers Association, which specializes in horror and "dark fantasy" and seeks to "foster a greater appreciation of dark fantasy among the general public." If you watch daytime television, you probably think that we're just about maxed out on dark fantasy. This website proves it's not so. Here you'll find lots about the world of horror writing, including a recommended reading list, information about and recipients of the Bram Stoker Awards for the past nine years, descriptions of members-only anthologies, a decent FAQ on the subject of literary agents, and some historical background on the group.

Investigative Writers and Editors (IRE)

http://www.ire.org

A strong sense of justice pervades this highly useful website. Investigative reporters are linked by a sense of outrage and ire, this website explains, making the group's name extremely apt. Its purpose is to help investigative reporters avoid "reinventing the wheel" every time they are assigned a story. An online database allows you to search for previously published stories about any given journalistic topic; the database currently contains 10,000 stories. Copyright restrictions prevent the posting of these stories on the site, but you can order fax or photocopy versions via e-mail (you'll find instructions at the site).

Incidentally, when you're typing in their Web address, keep in mind that the URL says "ire" and not "iwe."

National Association of Science Writers

http://www.nasw.org/

This organization fights for "the free flow of science information," and its website is extremely useful to anyone interested in reading about the reporting of science. You can find tips, resources, calls for information, recommendations and precautions for reaching science writers via e-mail or publishing on the Web, and membership information. You can also read or subscribe to the mailing lists, the main topic of which at the time of our visit was the "Inglefinger rule," the *New England Journal of Medicine*'s rule embargoing information in its pages until time of publication. Useful for anyone who writes about science.

National Writers Union

http://www.nwu.org

This leading writers' group, affiliated with the AFL-CIO, fights for authors' rights in all aspects of publishing—book, electronic, and journalism. The NWU offers contract advice, as well as information on electronic rights, free expression issues, copyright, and a host of other issues essential to the lives of writers. Members may use a database of information about literary agents. At their website you'll find essays and documents related to authors' rights, including excellent essays on the business aspects of publishing online. You'll also find a calendar listing local chapter events, discussions, and lectures across the country. The website also contains information on grievances with publishers, ongoing NWU projects, recent awards, and excellent links to over 350 useful sites for writers.

The NWU provides medical and dental insurance to writers—this is one of the few places where freelance writers have access to first-class, reasonably priced medical and dental insurance. The insurance is a benefit of the NWU's connection with the United Automobile Workers.

Newspaper Guild

http://www.dcarolco.com/tng

The basics about the Newspaper Guild, the union that represents writers and other employees at more than 200 media outlets in the United States. The website is attractive and offers a brief history of the organization and the essentials about how the guild works. This could be a wonderful site with a lot of history about newswriters and the news business, but right now you get the who, what, where, and when. With links at the time of our visit to about half a dozen related labor sites.

Society for Technical Communicators

http://heron.tc.clarkson.edu/

Clarkson University students and staff maintain this attractive website, which offers technical writers a place to interact, a notice board listing résumés (you may add yours), an e-mail address list, and a "Communicator's Forum" where lonely tech writers the world over talk to each other in their own particular language. You'll also find a few, not many, excerpts from their journal, *Technical Communication.*

Women's National Book Association

http://www.bookbuzz.com/wnbanyc.htm

A nationwide organization including authors, editors, publicists, booksellers, librarians, and others in the book business. The New York chapter, whose home page this is, sponsors nine events a year featuring top individuals in publishing, such as the editor of *The New York Times* book review and leading agents and authors. Panel discussions with Q&A.

Writer's Guild of America—East

http://www.wgaeast.org/html

How WGA Members Can Get Free Hollywood News Every Day

The east coast branch of the Writers' Guild. Its members work as freelance movie and television writers and are on staff at every level of television and radio news and entertainment. This site offers information about the guild, its services, its history, and links to many news, labor, government, economy, and women's issue sites. This site has a script registration service for members. Script registration is highly recommended—in Hollywood, ideas get stolen all the time. It's easier to purloin an idea than a book-length manuscript. That's why film and TV writers need more protection than novelists and short story writers.

Writer's Guild of America—West

http://www.wga.org/members/SB.html

Features include e-mail interviews with top writers and producers; "Overheard at the Commissary"—writers talking about writers; "Tools of the Trade" listing research Web links, experts, and more; news of the guild; and excerpts online from the guild's newsletter. Those articles currently include "The Ultimate Screenwriting Software Review," "Who Are Those Nielsens, Anyway?" and "Literary Agents: The View From the Other Side." Some features are just for Writers Guild members. But for those lucky devils (okay, I admit it, I am one): a daily "Studio Briefing," the monthly calendar of events, and film society schedule.

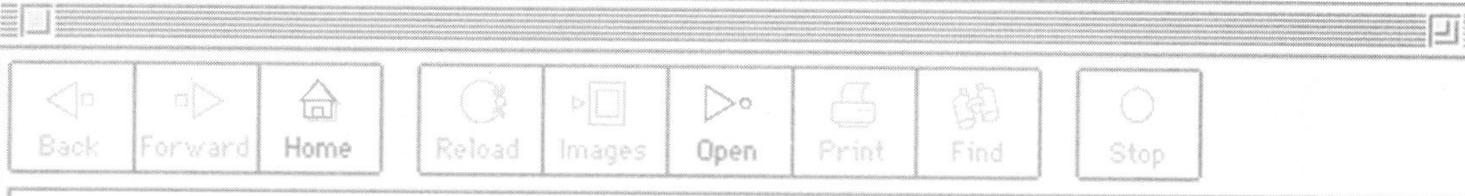

CHAPTER FOUR

PUBLISHING HOUSES

The major publishers, with only a few exceptions noted below, do not yet know what to make of the Internet. This section lists links to publishers' home pages around the world and provides a few examples of what major publishers and small presses are currently doing on the Web. I originally intended to list and review for you each website of each major publisher; but, frankly, they all look pretty much the same. They're glossy and expensive looking, they have similar features (press releases about a few authors, some articles, an order form) and they don't have nearly as much life as, say, the average poetry site maintained by an individual. This will change with time. Other houses will follow the lead of Penguin and Macmillan, which have the most interesting sites that I've found among the majors. In the meantime, as they say, do drop in.

LISTS OF PUBLISHING HOUSES

Association of American University Publishers

http://aaup.pupress.princeton.edu/

It's academic: You can find any academic publisher, text, or any author by visiting this page. Search engines allow you to search the entire AAUP database or the individual catalog of any single academic publisher. With links to many other academic press resources.

Internet Book Fair

http://www.bookfair.com/welcome/pindex

A home for home pages of publishers. This one's got some real money behind it, judging from the advertisers. Bantam-Doubleday-Dell was sponsoring the page when I visited. You can search for publishers by name or keyword.

Publishers

http://www.freenet.vcu.edu/education/literature/publishers.html

As I wrote at the beginning of this chapter, the top publishers, with a few exceptions, haven't really figured out what the Web is good for. The largest sites all sort of look the same—with attractive graphics, information on new titles, a few interviews, and order forms—but they don't break ground or really stand out one from the other. Rather than provide repetitious reviews, here's a collection of links to all the top publishers and some smaller ones, so you can shop and compare.

RECOMMENDED

Publishers on the Internet

http://www.faxon.com/internet/publishers/pubs.html

An amazing resource: thousands of publishers around the world, listed alphabetically, with links to their home pages. An extraordinarily useful site for authors, agents, librarians, and anyone else who wants quick and easy Internet access to virtually any publisher on the planet.

RECOMMENDED

Publishers' Catalogs Home Page

http://www.lights.com/publisher/

A monster site offering links to hundreds of publishers around the globe. You'll find the powerful and the obscure, academic presses, specialty houses, every publisher imaginable. You can also find publishers listed by country, including places like Japan, Turkey, Australia, and Singapore. Ideal for an author or publishing house looking to sell foreign rights. The "biographies" of the publishers give you their history and current list. An invaluable service. You'll also find publishers arranged by topic, such as "Academic," "Computer," and "Scientific/Technical/Medical." Also, there is a search engine, if you know the name of the publisher but can't find the Web address. Brought to you by Northern Lights Internet Solutions Ltd., Saskatoon, Canada. Publishers are invited to place their catalogs on this website.

EXAMPLES OF PUBLISHERS' WEBSITES

Avon Books

http://www.AvonBooks.com/

Find out about Avon's latest books along with limited information about their author appearances. An attractive and professional looking website.

Bantam-Doubleday-Dell

http://www.bdd.com

The latest books, of course, along with tour information for their authors and links to BDD authors' e-mail addresses and personal Web pages.

Blue Heron Publishing

http://www.teleport.com/~bhp/

Blue Heron, a publisher based in Hillsboro, Oregon, specializes in books that aid writers. Among their titles: *The Fine Art of Technical Writing, Nonfiction Book Proposals Anyone Can Write, Artists' and Writers' Colonies,* and *Writing Across Cultures.* They also publish some high-quality fiction. Under their resources section you'll find excellent information for online writers, including an extremely useful essay entitled "How to Prepare a Manuscript for Electronic Submission." You can go directly to that essay by visiting *http://www.teleport.com/~bhp/r3_DocPrep.html.* The site is especially useful for educators, who constitute a major market for Blue Heron's books. Each featured book, incidentally, gets its own most attractively designed Web page, making this website a model for other publishers.

Harlequin Books

http://www.romance.net

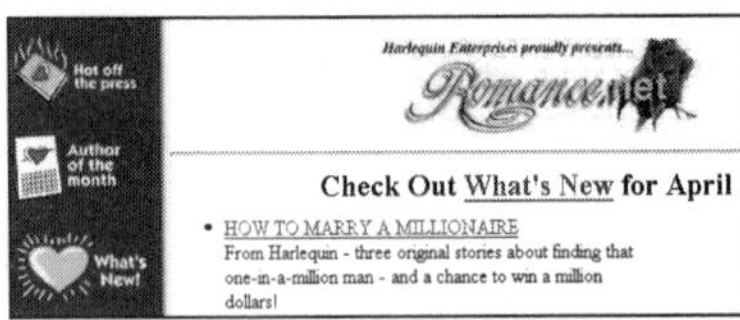

I can explain romance novels to you, in case you're not an aficionado. They're all about getting a grip on men who have one-syllable first names like "Girk" and "Blang" and "Klog" and making them shave. If you have any more questions about romance novels, or if you'd like links to the home pages of dozens of their authors, or if you want your horoscope read, drop in. You'll also find excerpts from "I Can Fix It Myself" by Susie Tompkins in the "Susie's Helpful Hints" archive.

Macmillan Books

http://www.mcp.com/

An attractive website, one of whose special features allows you to do a "supersearch" on any book-related topic. You type in your search request and the website performs the search on a number of different Internet search engines like Lycos and Yahoo!. This saves you the trouble of searching a book-related topic in each of the various search engines, one by one.

Penguin Books

http://www.penguin.com/

Information about forthcoming books from America's fourth largest publisher. The usual major house features, with one excellent feature: "The Reading Room," which offers sample chapters, updated biweekly, of new books from all of Penguin's imprints, including Penguin, Viking, and Putnam.

Reed Reference Publishing

http://www.reedref.com/

Reed publishes many of the leading reference books on writing, including *Books in Print*, *Books Out-of-Print*, and *Ulrich's International Periodicals Directory*. You can learn about purchasing or subscribing online to these excellent reference works or you can gain access for free to the online version of *Books Out of Print*.

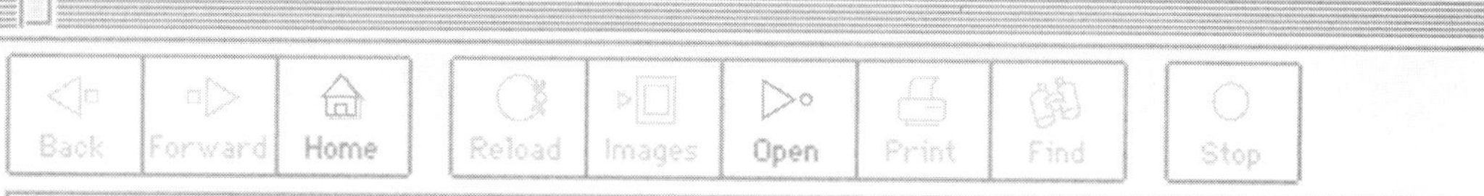

CHAPTER FIVE

WRITERS' CONFERENCES AND GROUPS

More and more writers' conferences are taking advantage of the Internet to find attendees and attract members. But if you want to find the largest number of writers' conferences, you really want to get a copy of the book *The Guide to Writers Conferences*, fourth edition, published by ShawGuides of Coral Gables, Florida. This book lists complete information for 344 writers' conferences, workshops, seminars, residencies, retreats, and organizations around the world and is the most comprehensive guide to writers' conferences that I've ever seen. Interestingly, for a book about writers, it does not name its own author. I mention the book because this is a situation where the Internet simply hasn't caught up with the resources currently available in print. Nonetheless, to show you what already exists on the Internet—and to encourage more conferences and groups to go online—we're happy to offer you the following sites.

WRITERS' CONFERENCES

American Library Association

http://www.ala.org/alaevents/annual96/ny_home.html

The ALA is a massive gathering of librarians that takes over the Javits Center in New York for four days each July. The latest in shushing technologies; acrimonious debates on whether "Mc" should be shelved before M or after Mac; and the biggest event of all: the librarians divide into two teams, the Dewey Decimal System Devils versus the Library of Congress Cougars, and compete in Due Date–card stamping, book alphabetizing, and speed reshelving. I wouldn't miss it for the world. Seriously, this is one of the major events in bookdom and you can read all about it here.

Clarion West Writers Workshop

http://www.halcyon.com/anitar/clar97.html

If you're a writer preparing for a career in science fiction or fantasy writing, you might want to consider this annual six-week workshop, held at Seattle Central Community College in Seattle, Washington, every June and July. The 1997 instructors include Elizabeth Hand, Michael Bishop, Samuel R. Delany, and Beth Meacham. To apply, offer them one or two short stories and an application fee; information is available at the website.

Southwest Writers Workshop

http://www.us1.net/SWW/

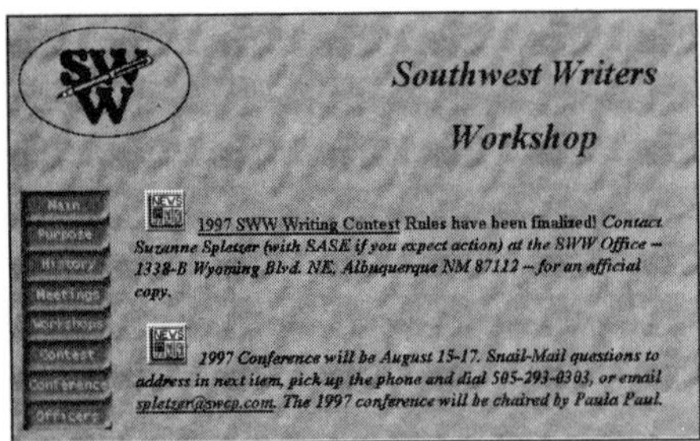

This group holds an annual conference each August in Albuquerque, New Mexico, where you can meet many top agents, editors, and authors in workshops and social settings. The group holds a writing contest in conjunction with the workshop, makes low-cost health and dental insurance available to members, provides access to a credit union, and enables members to join the Albuquerque

Press Club. Its 1,100 members write in all genres; about a quarter of the group has been published. Get to know them, join, or learn about the conference here.

Surrey Writers' Conference

http://ourworld.compuserve.com/homepages/Ed_Griffin/

Surrey is halfway between Vancouver, British Columbia (one of the world's most beautiful cities), and the U.S. border; each October, there you'll find a big-time annual conference featuring top authors, editors, booksellers, magazine editors, computer and Internet providers, and writers' organizations. Also a "mini conference for younger writers." Workshops, one-on-one conferences, and a trade show highlight the event; for more information or a brochure, visit the website.

University of Iowa Summer Writing Festival

http://www.uiowa.edu/%7Eiswfest/time.html

One of America's leading writing programs offers you the chance to attend summer workshops, classes, and special events. This well-designed and quite thorough website gives you all the information you need about the nature of the program, the genres (fiction, poetry, nonfiction, writing for children, screenwriting and playwrighting, and something called "genre benders"), registration materials, and everything you need to prepare for "your time in Iowa." Several dozen workshops offer you time with top writing instructors and motivated students; it's all waiting for you at this website.

W.R.I.T.E. (Writers' Retreat on Interactive Technology and Equipment)

http://www.cstudies.ubc.ca/write/write.html

This annual conference in lovely Vancouver, British Columbia, offers writers the chance to learn about using audio and video tools in their work. Typical seminar subjects include "Demystifying Interactive Media and the Information Superhighway" and an "Internet Publishing Workshop."

Writers Roundtable Conference

http://project-iowa.org/WRC/

This annual conference, meeting in Dallas in April, 1997, features top authors, editors, agents, and publishers and runs on a two-track basis: One track is for professional writers; the other is for writers who are getting started in the field. Choose your track and sign on here.

WRITERS' GROUPS

Bay Area Writers Groups

http://www.enclave.org/write

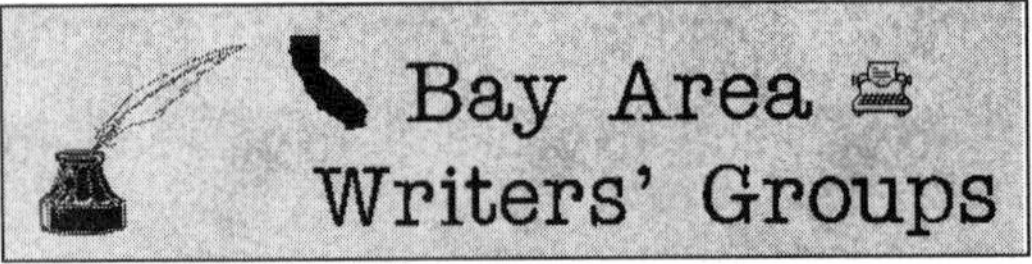

Thirty writers' groups in the San Francisco Bay Area list their meeting times and locations, interests, level of experience, fees, contact names, and phone numbers or e-mail addresses. Lots of sci fi, some screenwriters, something for everyone. This is a great service—one that writers' groups in other cities might want to emulate.

Writers Groups Around the World

http://www.writepage.com/groups.htm

What a brilliant idea: an international listing of writers' groups, organized by region of the United States or by country. With information on the nature of the group; where and when they meet; dues, conferences, or publications; and names, addresses, phone numbers, and where available, e-mail or Web links for the contact people. You can join the Rogue Writers of Murphy, Oregon; the New Age–oriented Word Goddesses of Irvine, Texas; or L'Atelier du scenario in Paris, which concentrates on screenplays. Post your group, find one to join, or start your own. This is what the Internet is for—helping like-minded folks meet each other in person and not just isolating themselves ("cybernating") behind their screens at home.

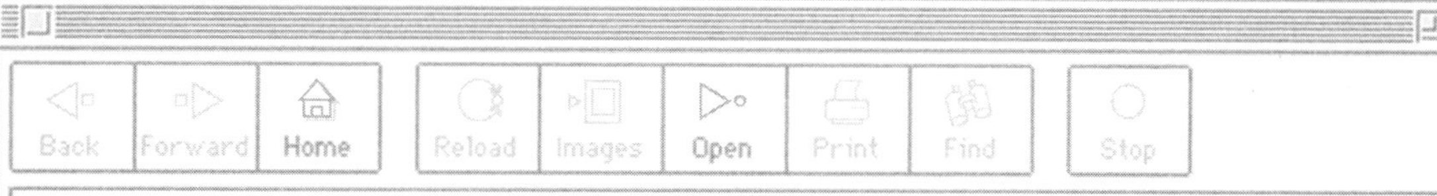

CHAPTER SIX

AWARDS AND PRIZES

Wondering who won what award this year, or in some previous year? Looking for something good to read in your favorite field? The Internet makes it easy for you to find the winners of awards and prizes for adult, young adult, and genre fiction. Some of the sites listed here have links to bookstores, allowing you to preview and order the book from the comfort of your computer desk. From the Pulitzer to the Prix Goncourt of France, you can look it up right here.

Hugo Awards

http://www.city-net.com/~lmann/awards/hugos/

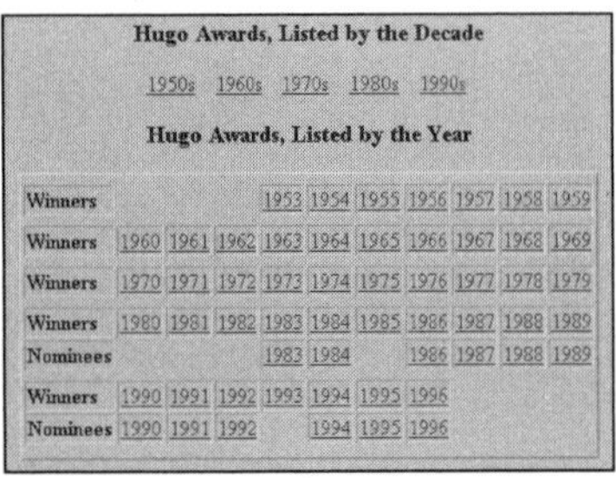

Hugo Awards, Listed by the Decade

1950s 1960s 1970s 1980s 1990s

Hugo Awards, Listed by the Year

Winners				1953	1954	1955	1956	1957	1958	1959
Winners	1960	1961	1962	1963	1964	1965	1966	1967	1968	1969
Winners	1970	1971	1972	1973	1974	1975	1976	1977	1978	1979
Winners	1980	1981	1982	1983	1984	1985	1986	1987	1988	1989
Nominees				1983	1984		1986	1987	1988	1989
Winners	1990	1991	1992	1993	1994	1995	1996			
Nominees	1990	1991	1992		1994	1995	1996			

Science fiction's greatest prize; you can look up the winners by decade or by year at this site. This is a list of winners. If you want to learn more about the authors, visit the Science Fiction/Fantasy/Horror section of this book or visit the hyperlinks offered at this site.

Of related interest: Science Fiction/Fantasy/Horror

Literary Prizes: Fiction

http://www-stat.wharton.upenn.edu/~siler/litlists.edu

Who won the Pulitzer Prize for Literature, the National Book Award, the Whitbread Prize, the Prix Goncourt, the Nobel Prize? Find out here, or read a *Times Literary Supplement* article, "International Books of the Year," in which writers select the books that impressed them most in the past year. Also a "Professor's guilt list," which "attempts to help an English major find out if he/she is qualified to apply for a grad program." I've read very few of these recommended books, but now that I live in Los Angeles, I don't feel any guilt at all. I am disappointed, however, that there's nothing by Fabio on the list.

Mystery Awards

http://freenet.vcu.edu/education/literature/mystaward.html

Here you'll find winners, nominees, and a best-books list for the Edgar Awards, the highest praise for a mystery novel, awarded by the Mystery Writers of America. You'll also find the winners of the Anthony, Shamus, Macavity, Tangled Web, and Arthur Ellis awards.

Of related interest: Mystery Writing

National Book Award

http://www.wordsworth.com/awards/nba.cgi?UID=10105014210478

Authors and titles of the winners of the National Book Award, with links that allow you to order the books at a discount from Wordsworth Books of Cambridge, Massachusetts. When I was in short pants, I used to gaze at the paperback section of said bookstore and tell myself, "Someday . . ."

The National Book Awards: Fiction

[Help] [Checkout Counter] [Catalogs] [Awards] [Author Events] [Do A Search]
[CG Home] [Ask WordsWorth] [Show VirtualBag] [Home]

This is a listing of the National Book Award Winners since 1969.

Not all these books are in print, and some are available as special orders.
Please check with us on the availability of any title you are interested in.

The Availability Key:

The availablity reflects *U.S. Books in Print*.

1996	Andrea Barrett	Ship Fever and Other Stories
1995	Philip Roth	Sabbath's Theater
1994	William Gaddis	Frolic of his Own
1993	E. Anne Proulx	The Shipping News
1992	Cormac McCarthy	All the Pretty Horses
1991	Norman Rush	Mating
1990	Charles Johnson	Middle Passage
1989	John Casey	Spartina

Newbery and Caldecott Book Awards

http://www.bookwire.com/awards/childrens96.html

The two leading awards for children's writing. You'll find the honorees, the five runners-up, and the *Publishers Weekly* reviews for each of these titles.

Of related interest: Young Adult, Middle Grade, and Children's Writing

Parents' Choice Awards

http://family.starwave.com:80/reviews/pchoice/awards1/

Parents' Choice, established in 1978, publishes a nonprofit consumer guide to children's books, toys, video, audio, computer programs, TV, magazines, rock, and pop. At this website you can find its choices for 1995; the 1996 awards are presumably on their way. Subjects include picture books, paperbacks, story books, and other media.

Pulitzer Prizes

http://www.pulitzer.org/

Welcome to the Pulitzer Prizes World Wide Web site, containing the works and profiles of Prize winners past and present.

Works and profiles of current Pulitzer winners, a searchable archive, and a brief history of the Pulitzer Prize. The Pulitzers were first awarded in 1917; information about pre-1995 winners was under construction at my last visit. Also background about the jurors, including professional affiliation, favorite sports car, number of Swiss bank accounts, and favorite vacation spot, in case you would like to bribe them. (I'm kidding, I'm kidding.)

CHAPTER SEVEN

BOOK FAIRS

Most people in the publishing industry have not yet begun to harness the power of the Internet. This certainly includes book fair organizers. Soon every book fair will have a massive website of its own; in the meantime, you can find many in the first two entries in this section. If you have always wanted your books or your publishing company to have a presence at international fairs, be certain to visit the website of the Overseas Book Service below.

American Book Association—Events

http://bookweb.org/events/75.html

This aspect of the BookWeb website of the American Book Association offers you information on upcoming book fairs and festivals across the United States. You can also follow links to Web pages for specific events to get more information and to register. In some cases, e-mail addresses for event organizers are included. Speakers, events, special interest items for kids—they're all listed here.

Book Fairs and Festivals

http://www.bookfair.com/Fairs/index.html

Zimbabwe, San Francisco, Bologna, New Delhi, Taipei, Seattle—links to book fairs and festivals in these and other cities. You can learn about the festivals and their specialties (for example, Bologna is a childrens' book fair); you can get schedules, prices, and registration information.

Children's Book Festival

http://ocean.st.usm.edu/~dajones/CBF.htm

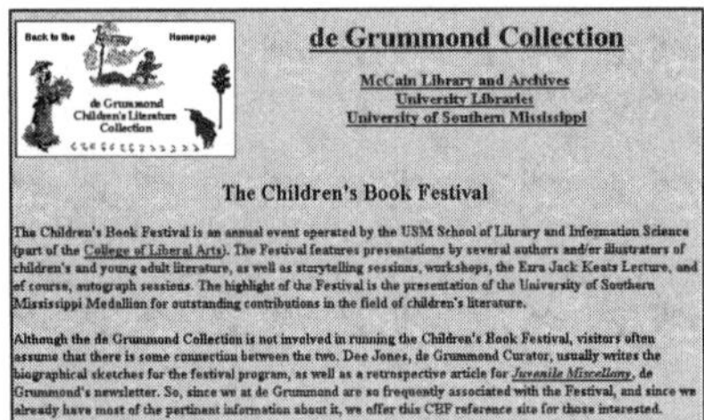

A harbinger of spring since 1968, this book festival is sponsored by the de Grummond collection of children's literature and takes place on the University of Southern Mississippi campus. It features presentations by leading authors, illustrators, editors, critics, and educators. Storytelling sessions, workshops, lectures, and autograph sessions are also among the events.

Overseas Book Service—International Book Fairs

http://www.rio.com/~ross/obs.html

Want to get international exposure without having to spend a fortune? This company, located in Bazzano, Italy, organizes a collective book and multimedia exhibit at international book fairs. Their 1997 schedule includes London in March, the Children's Book Fair in Bologna in April, the Warsaw International Book Fair in May, and Frankfurt in October. They'll display your titles, enter you in the fair guide, take orders, and much more. Get the lowdown at their website and send them e-mail if you're interested.

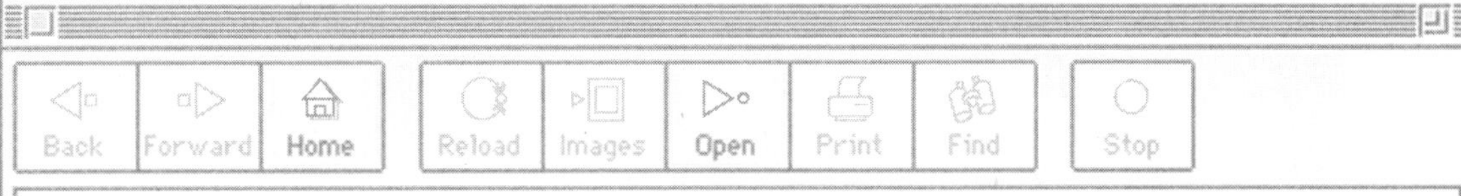

CHAPTER EIGHT

BOOKSELLERS ONLINE

You've been using computers to write books for some time. Now you can use your computer to help you buy books—new, used, hard-to-find, out of print, academic, antiquarian, or rare. These sites take you to traditional bookstores around the world that use cutting-edge technology to let you search their entire stock so that you can browse at home. And they also take you to a new breed of bookstore (the biggest and most amazing of which is amazon.com): online bookstores that exist only in cyberspace—and because they don't have the limitations of actual bookstores, they can carry 20 times the books that even the superstores can. You can shop with a credit card and complete your entire order online.

Amazon.com

RECOMMENDED

http://www.amazon.com

Amazon.com offers you more than a million books. You can not only order the books online, you can also have them gift wrapped and send them anywhere on the planet. A million titles is roughly the equivalent of 20 book superstores, all at one website. *Books in Print,* I'm told, lists about 1.4 million titles; you can get the overwhelming majority of them here. You'll also get a 30 percent discount on *New York Times* bestsellers and 10 percent off most other books every day (with deeper discounts on their favorites). Clickable lists show you which books were recently mentioned in various magazines or radio or TV broadcasts, reviews, a free personal notification service to let you know when your favorite author has written a new book, and the opportunity to sell their books from your website as an Amazon.com associate. What an amazing development this bookstore is.

Blackwell's on the Internet

http://www.blackwell.co.uk/bookshops/

The "world's finest academic bookshop" offers at its website a BookSearch; a "tour" of its Oxford bookshop; a searchable rare-books department; catalogs; bestseller lists; and, each month, a focus on a particular genre with recommended new titles. When I visited, they were reviewing bibliographies and offered a most thoughtful selection of books. Well worth your time if you're wondering what to read next.

Book Lovers

http://www.xs4all.nl/~pwessel/

From the Netherlands, here's a selection of useful sites with links to the Antiquarian Booksellers of America Association, mailing lists for bibliophiles, Conservation OnLine, bookbinding, book arts, and book history resources on the Web.

Booksellers of All Kinds

http://www.bookwire.com/index/booksellers.html

Online booksellers in 16 categories, from antiquarian, audio, business, and children's, through science fiction, specialty, travel, and university. With annotated links to dozens of bookstores around the world.

Bookstacks Unlimited, Inc.

http://www.books.com/scripts/news.exe

This online bookseller offers over 400,000 titles, most or all of which come at a 15 percent discount. What makes the home page fun is a "Book of Days" revised daily, offering audio interviews with authors, a poetry corner, information about books, quotations about writing, and more. "Literary Lore" lets you know whose birthday it is in bookdom. With interesting links to other publishing- and book-related sites.

BookZone

http://www.bookzone.com

This online bookstore sells titles that other stores might not carry. Over 500 publishers' catalogs are represented here, and their titles are listed alphabetically, by dozens of subject headings, and through a search menu. They do an especially good job with audiobooks and have a wide variety of intriguing audio titles for your enjoyment.

Borders Books-Music-Cafe

http://www.borders.com

Reviews, locations of stores, selected nationwide events, and plans for an online ordering service at this attractively designed home page. The "What We're Recommending" section is worth your time. Borders people know books, and this aspect of their Web page offers selections from their staffs across the fruited plain.

Business and Computer Bookstore

http://www.bcb.com

A real-live bookstore—actually a chain of bookstores in and around Pennsylvania—specializing in computer books. You can search their database by topic or even download their catalogs, all of which had been updated in the month prior to our visit. Communications, PC, Macintosh, Technical and Programming, and many other categories. This site has links to Ken's Computer Museum and a number of other intriguing computer-oriented sites.

Computer Literacy

http://www.clbooks.com

The technology-minded book buyer will find science and technology books, reviews of books, and news of in-store events at this bicoastal bookstore's wonderful website. A search engine allows you to look for books by field of interest or keyword. Reviews of new books, information about upcoming titles, and the ability to order books via e-mail make this site essential to any master of science. This site has information on employment opportunities at their stores. This is the website of an actual, as opposed to strictly virtual, bookstore.

Computer Manuals

http://www.compman.co.uk

A lot more than computer manuals are available at this site, the home page of one of Europe's largest computer bookstores. You'll find reviews of the newest computer books, recommendations, a search engine, and a "Features" section that shows you what you need to know about the latest trends in hardware and software. Find links to hardware and software companies, games, programming sites, and lots more about British and European computing.

Feminist Bookstores

http://www.igc.apc.org/women/bookstores/

This site lists hundreds of feminist and women's bookstores across the United States and Canada, organized by state or province, and provides address, phone, and, if available, e-mail and Web links. This site offers a list of recommended books of interest to women and "a short rant on the importance of supporting women's bookstores." There are lists of links for women's issues and alternative sexuality, and links to an index of worldwide feminist and gay and lesbian booksellers.

Of related interest: Women Writers' Resources

Independent Reader

http://www.independentreader.com/

Every successful author knows the importance of independent booksellers, whose recommendations are taken extremely seriously by their legions of customers. Here you can find suggestions from 12 of the leading independent booksellers in America, including the Tattered Cover in Denver, Cody's Bookstore in Berkeley, the Harvard Book Store in Cambridge, and the Hungry Mind in St. Paul. Each store lists five books per month; you'll also find an index to the combined lists and book comments from the readers. Find links to the bookstores' home pages. An excellent idea and a great way to find good books to read or to give.

Internet Book Fair

http://www.bookfair.com/Booksellers/booksellers.html

This site provides links to about 25 booksellers who sell over the Internet; listings are limited to online bookstores and to publishers that publish more than their own works. The stores are located everywhere from Irvine, California, to Iceland, and the listings are divided into three sections (at this time): general catalogs; scientific, technical, and computer; and special interest.

The Internet Bookshop—United Kingdom

http://www.bookshop.com.uk

This British bookseller claims to be "the largest online bookshop in the world," a boast the folks at amazon.com might like to discuss with them. The site lets you order any of 912,000 books (at the time of our visit) and search for books by subject. If you're an Anglophile, you'll find many titles of interest to you and also works on British literature and crafts. Subjects include antiques, architecture, classics, gardening, history, natural history, sports and hobbies, travel, and more. You can also check out (and order from) a list of British bestsellers.

It's so gosh-darned British, as in this excerpt from the bestselling novel, *Death Is Now My Neighbor*, by Colin Dexter: "As he drove his chief down to Kidlington, Lewis returned the conversation to where it had begun. 'You haven't told me what you think about this fellow Owens—the dead woman's next door neighbour.' 'Death is always the next-door neighbour,' said Morse sombrely."

Gotta love it.

Intertain.com

http://www.intertain.com/store/IBIC

This online bookstore offers over half a million books for sale; you can search by topic. You can also find reviews and essays on every subject and genre of book at its related site, the Internet Book Information Center.

U.S. Booksellers

http://www.ambook.org/bookweb/sellerlist/bystate.html

A searchable database of all U.S. bookstores. You can search by state or by keyword in the bookstore's name. A service of the American Booksellers Association.

Virtual Book Shop

http://virtual.bookshop.com/booksellers.html

Like first editions? Like early printed books from 1500 to 1850? Like browsing through used and antiquarian bookshops? Then you'll turn virtual cartwheels over the Virtual Book Shop, which mentions the specialties and lists the inventory of dozens of privately owned bookstores in the United States, Canada, England, and even Italy. Here's how it works: You can enter author, title, or subject in their catalog. I typed in **Damon Runyon** and found three titles: Damon Runyon's "Poems For Men" in a 1947 first edition, "VG+, in dustwrapper that is chipped at extremities but still bright and Runyonesque" for $40, and two biographies. I clicked on the first edition and chose "save." By clicking on "review order" I learned that I was in the process of ordering this book from Michael J. Toth, Bookseller in Springtown, Pennsylvania. If I really wanted to buy the book, I could have gone to an online order form, and typed in my e-mail address, actual address, and Visa number, and Mr. Toth instantaneously would know that I'd ordered the book. I ask you, how cool is the Internet?

WebCube Bookstore

http://www.webcube.com/

This site is a little odd—it's an online bookstore with only one or two titles, most from small presses, in each category. It moves cases of unsalable books at large discounts. It offers useful essays on subjects like publishing scams in its "Author's Corner"; and offers rights to unpublished manuscripts like "Raising Beef for Fun and Profit." The classified section offers two items: billiard posters and billiard videos. Well, that's the Internet for you. A little of this and a little of that.

CHAPTER NINE

COPYRIGHT

The Internet has been described as "the world's largest copying machine." We as readers may be quite excited about the vast amount of information and literature now at our fingertips. We as writers may be a bit less excited when we realize that virtually no writer whose work appears on the Internet is ever paid for it.

The future of copyright protection is one of the most important issues currently facing writers. The sites in this section offer everything you need to know about traditional copyright protection and also set forth the perils, pitfalls, and means of protection for writers in cyberspace.

Association of American Publishers

http://www.publishers.org/copyright/index.html

This leading publisher's organization works to educate librarians, educators, and the public about copyright law. You can read their position papers on document delivery and scanning here. This site is for those who are deeply interested in the topic; people seeking information about the basics of copyright registration and protection should visit some of the websites listed below.

Authors Registry

http://www.vmedia/com/alternate/shannon/authorsguild.html

The Authors Guild, a leading U.S. writers' group, has launched a means by which authors can be properly compensated for their work. Authors who register their work here make it easier for film producers, foreign publishers, and paperback publishers to find them, buy rights, and pay them. Nearly 15,000 authors are already registered. Find out how to get protected and paid . . . here.

The Basics About Copyright Registration

http://www.asja/org/copyright.htm

Freelance writers interested in a quick and useful summary of U.S. laws regarding copyright protection and registration can tune in here. A service of the American Society of Journalists and Authors.

Copyright Clearance Center Online

RECOMMENDED

http://www.copyright.com/

One of the most important sites for authors, for educators, and for publishers. The Copyright Clearance Center contains databases of books and other publications. If you want to photocopy pages for any reason, you can get permission from the author via the CCC. Educators, businesses, and others who fail to secure copyright permissions before they photocopy and distribute copyrighted works are violating the law. The CCC offers a simple and easy way to get those permissions.

How important is this to authors? One recent case involved a multinational corporation that bought one copy of a scientist's book and made 45,000 copies for its employees around the world. Thanks to the CCC, that author was properly compensated by the corporation. In many ways, the CCC is the writer's equivalent of ASCAP, the organization that protects the rights of musicians. Visit this site, register your published works, and stay informed about your rights as an author.

RECOMMENDED

The Copyright Website

http://www.benedict.com/

Copyright information in concise terms with information on registration; what you need to know about copyright infringement; Internet issues; and the "fair use" doctrine, which allows you to use a small portion of a copyrighted work in certain circumstances—if you provide proper credit. You'll also be able to hear audio comparisons of musical works that approached or crossed the copyright line, learn the meaning of public domain ("where copyrights go to die"), and find other source documents and related links. This is an extremely important issue for writers, and this website absolutely deserves your time.

RECOMMENDED

Library of Congress

http://lcWeb.loc.gov/copyright/

Why not go right to the source? The Library of Congress home page offers you everything you've always wanted to know about copyright law. You'll get the basics about copyright: how to register, what protection means, how to get copyright information by fax, and lots, lots more. You can even download copyright registration forms for free.

National Creative Registry Online

http://www.ncronline.com

Sounds like an intriguing idea: You can register up to 1MB of your writing for six years for $18.95 and thus provide yourself with documented proof that you wrote it on such and such a date. This company claims to offer the "exact same protection" as the Writer's Guild registration service "for less money and longer terms." It's certainly easy enough to do—you upload them a text file and give them a credit card number and they fire back a registration number; no one else has access to the file.

It seems straightforward, but I would rather spend my $18.95 on a new book.

Why?

I've got three concerns about companies like this, based on my experience as (1) a writing teacher, (2) an attorney, and (3) a computer user.

As a writing teacher, I can tell you flat out that the number-one concern of fledging writers is how to keep their work from being stolen. This question looms much larger in most new writers' minds than the question "How do I make this piece of writing extremely good?" The movie industry is famous for people stealing each other's work, but in books, it virtually never happens. I'll repeat that in case you went into a trance state: In the publishing world, it's unbelievably rare to find people stealing each other's stuff. So you don't have to worry in the first place.

But if you're like most writers, you'll ignore me and say "I want protection anyway."

In that case, I'll put on my lawyer hat and tell you that copyright protection of any kind only makes a difference if you can afford to hire a lawyer and go to court. As this can run into tens of thousands of dollars, you've got to ask yourself, "Even if I register something somewhere, and if the million-to-one thing happens and somebody steals it, how much protection do I really have?" Sadly, in America, you get all the justice you can afford.

Now I'll speak with my computer-user hat on. Remember that hard disks, floppies, and everything else crashes eventually. I would not rely solely on electronic storage for anything I might have to go to court over. Print out your manuscript, go to the Library of Congress site (it's listed in his section), download and print out Form TX, send them the manuscript and the $25, and rest easy—knowing that Uncle Sam is standing guard over your work.

Or better still, forget all about protecting your work and just concentrate on making it so good that every publisher will want to publish it and every reader will want to buy it. Isn't that what it's all about, anyway?

Of course, you may agree with Vladimir Nabokov, who quoted Dostoyevsky to the effect that "I write for myself and I publish to make a living." Either way. Just have fun writing and don't spend too much of your hard-earned cash on "protecting" your work.

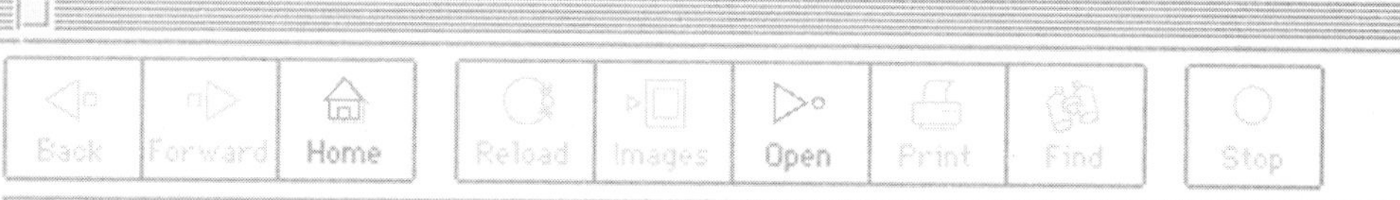

CHAPTER TEN

EMPLOYMENT FOR WRITERS

These sites offer writers the greatest luxury of all—employment. Many offer from 10,000 to 250,000 jobs nationwide in all fields and include dozens or even 100 or more jobs for writers. Many of these positions are for technical writers but you'll find work in many different fields if you spend a little time with the various search engines. You tell the computers to which these sites link you what kind of writing you do and where you like to do it. You'll get information on jobs in your location. Some of the sites even allow you to apply for the job directly over the Internet. Visit each site regularly, as the listings change daily.

America's Job Bank

http://www.ajb.dni.us

This excellent free service is produced by the U.S. Department of Labor and offers over 250,000 job listings coast to coast. You can search the job database by keyword; I typed in **Writer or Writing** and got over 150 listings for employment for writers. Full time and part time work available here; you can also find paid writing internships if you're a student. Positions include mostly journalism, medical, scientific, and technical writing positions, but there were also intriguing listings for a TV writer in Maui, and a boating writer in southern Florida. You can also limit your search by state or by region of the country. Salary, benefits, and full job descriptions are all waiting for you here.

Bricolage

http://bricolage.bel-epa.com

You'll find employment opportunities for all kinds of writers at this site. Writers of nonfiction, journalism, business and technical writing, and even adult-oriented material can find jobs here.

Career Magazine

http://www.careermag.com

CAREERMagazine

Career Magazine is a magazine published on the Internet focussed on careers. You'll find articles about what employers can and cannot ask in interviews, from a legal point of view; advice on how to properly format your résumé when sending it to an Internet search engine; a column on managing your career and your life; and job openings, a forum on employment, and, of course, job listings. If you judge a commercial website by its advertisers, this one's doing something right. Advertisers include the big employment companies like Manpower. **Writer or Writing** netted about 150 jobs, almost entirely for technical writers. What did you expect—"Sr. Vice President/Haiku"?

CareerMosaic

http://www.careermosaic.com

This site lists about 15,000 jobs and twice as many résumés. Their search menu allows you to search by job title, by location, or by company. This site is international: click on the country where you'd like to work and let the search engine, called J.O.B.S., do the rest. **Writer or Writing** turned up about 40 positions around the United States, virtually all of which were technical writing positions. That's really what this site seems to be aimed at, judging from its sponsors, who are bigtime techie companies.

The "Online Job Fair" feature lets you travel directly to a "virtual job fair" sponsored by an employer like Intel or Martin Marietta. The corporation tells you about itself, lists available jobs, and offers you an e-mail form on which you can tell them about your education and work experience and thus get the hiring process started immediately. Obviously this is more for technical writers than for poets and novelists, but you never know.

CareerPath

http://www.careerpath.com

CareerPath offers over 125,000 jobs in all fields; they provide you with the classified ads from two dozen of America's largest newspapers. You can instantly find out what writing jobs are available in the *New York Times*, the *Denver Post*, the *Washington Post*, and the *Orlando Sentinel*, for example. You choose the newspaper and the field or fields you're interested in, and their speedy search engine will present you instantly with all relevant jobs. Plus a FAQ explaining to employers how and why to use the Internet to find job seekers.

Creative Freelancers Registry

http://www.ghgcorp.com/cfr/

Here you will find a Freelancers' Database of graphic designers, children's book designers, computer graphics people, imagery to film types, and writers of every sort: ad copy writers; conceptual writers; ghost writers; indexers; interviewers; journalists; and researchers, among other categories. "Ghost writers" was more the operative term as most of the categories were empty or had just one or a few writers or artists. So there's plenty of space for folks to come join in. This site is based in the Houston area, but since it's the Internet, y'all come and list yourselves from wherever you are.

E-Span

http://www.espan.com

E-Span, a commercial service for employers and job seekers, offers approximately 12,000 job listings searchable by keywords, company name, geographical area, educational level, or workplace level. **Writer or Writing** produced 538 jobs, most—but not all—of which are technical positions. Some are for copy writers and some are with mainstream publishing companies. Personality tests, résumé advice, and a section on special needs in the workplace make this a most useful employment information service for writers and for all job seekers.

Freelance Online

RECOMMENDED

http://www.freelanceonline.com/

Freelance writers can find work, an easy way to get their c.v. in front of countless employers, and good conversation about the pleasures and pitfalls of their line of work at this excellent site. At the time of our visit, it cost nothing for a freelance writer to post an extensive résumé, including client references, educational background, specialies, and links to one's own e-mail address or website. The freelance writer may choose any of these categories: freelance; interactive multimedia; broadcasting/video; writing; art-related; and production. Each category breaks down into clickable subgroups. Click on **Writing** and you'll find dozens of possibilities: medical, comedy, women's issues, technical, and marketing, to name just a few. The employment section lists dozens (at our visit) of jobs of all sorts for companies across the country. Where else but the Internet could a freelance writer find timely job listings for work with employers in Louisiana, New Hampshire, and Washington state, all in one easy-to-use location?

And there's more. A "resident accountant" lets you ask questions about tax and financial matters. An "open forum" offers discussion among freelancers. This site has "monster" potential all over it. Get your résumé and get on board.

Help Wanted USA

http://www.iccweb.com

This site is the brainchild of Gonyea and Associates, a firm that specializes in delivering information about careers and the workplace via computers. It offers 10,000 job listings, a place for your résumé, and lots and lots of career help online. An especially interesting feature is a "Career Analysis Service"—you download and answer over 100 questions about yourself and your work interests and personality. E-mail them the answers and for a small fee ($39.95) they'll run your answers through their computer and tell you what fields you may be best suited for. I tried it and found out that I should be a male model. Seriously, you might just learn something interesting about your career interests here.

The Monster Board

http://www.monster.com

Fifty thousand jobs are available via The Monster Board. This site should be of special interest to college students and people in their twenties because of the emphasis on "progressive" employers; entry-level positions; internship opportunities; and "cool works," including jobs in the great outdoors, national parks, cruise ships, and ski resorts. Actually, there's something romantic about being, say, a fire watcher in a national forest; it ought to give you plenty of time to write. Or to drink heavily. Dozens of National Parks are listed. I looked into the listing for Yosemite, here in California, and found dozens of job listings, both seasonal and year-round. I'm sure there are plenty of other attractive ways for young writers to get interesting day jobs that will give them much to write about and much time in which to write.

Online Career Center

http://www.occ.com

A smaller service listing approximately 30,000 jobs, Online Career Center lets you search for jobs by industry and location and also offers you a place to put your résumé in view of employers. You can even edit your résumé once you've posted it. A career advisory service is available, along with information on job fairs, diversity in the workplace, and related topics. There are also forums for job seekers and for college students to discuss the job market; and it's all free. When I punched in **Writer or Writing**, I found no less than 2,200 job openings! Most but not all postings are in technical and computer fields.

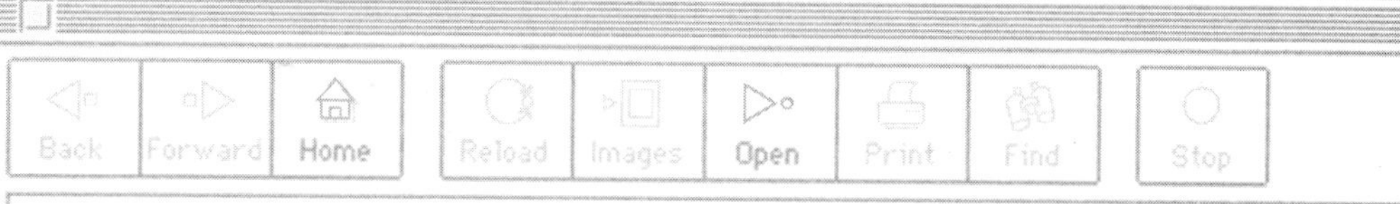

CHAPTER ELEVEN

ESSAYS ON WRITING AND PUBLISHING

These are the best essays on the Internet about the art, craft, and business of writing. You'll find fascinating information about the history of writing; how to make money as a freelance writer; what a good nonfiction book proposal looks like; whether self-publishing is right for you; how to write query letters; and much, much more. Dip into these sites and be prepared to learn a great deal about what it means to be a writer.

The Editorial Eye

http://www.eei-alex.com/eye/

A 12-page monthly newsletter published for the last 18 years in Alexandria, Virginia, a "resource for writers, editors, designers, project managers, communications specialists, and everyone else who cares about contemporary publishing practices." In other words, you. The "online sampler" here at the website offers examples of their articles, which discuss writing techniques; "efficient and tactful ways to edit others" (I e-mailed a copy of this to my publisher—think he'll get the hint? As if!); changes in grammar, usage, and publishing conventions; trends; and industry news. I let the site select an article at random, and I got "The Struggle for Gender-Free Language: Is It Over Yet?," a nicely written piece on the subject of hims and hers. Worth your time.

Freelance Writing: Frequently Asked Questions, with Marcia Yudkin

http://www.interlog.com/~ohi/inkspot/freelancefaq.html

Marcia Yudkin is one of America's leading experts on writing and publishing. She offers answers to the most commonly asked questions (Do I need a contract? How do I make contact with an editor? What's a query letter? How do I keep my work from being stolen?). Brought to you by Inkspot, which you'll find reviewed separately in Chapter 5, "Writers' Conferences and Groups."

Getting Started—The Real Facts

http://www.monash.com/writers.html

The Novelist's Workshop

Linda Barlow, bestselling novelist and president of the Romance Writers of America, gives you concise information about how to get started writing and publishing. If you want the truth, the whole truth, and nothing but the truth about agents, money, first-time writers, and other topics related to making your way in the publishing world, start here. Ms. Barlow also offers thoughtfully chosen links to other excellent websites.

Of related interest: Romance Writing

RECOMMENDED

Hungry Mind Review

http://www.bookwire.com/

A delightful and extremely useful site. The online equivalent of the *Hungry Mind Review,* a quarterly publication devoted to books and bookselling produced by the Hungry Mind, one of America's leading bookstores, located in St. Paul, Minnesota. Essays on the state of publishing and bookselling, reviews, articles about famous authors, and lists of "quirky bestsellers" are all delivered in an entertaining, well-written, and friendly manner. Also find interviews, poetry, information on writing for young adults, and previous issues in a searchable archive. This site is especially worthwhile to the new author seeking to get a sense of how the bookselling business really works.

RECOMMENDED

Inkspot

http://www.interlog.com/~ohi/inkspot/

An information-rich resource for the neophyte and the experienced pro alike. A "frequently asked questions" section tackles the basics—How do I get started? How do I get rid of writer's block? How do copyright laws apply to the Internet? How do I find a market for my work? But that's only the beginning. You'll find "Inklings," a free e-mail magazine for writers; writers' groups that allow writers to discuss craft; market information and classifieds offering links to publishers and information on jobs for writers;

and polls on topics like "What's the best piece of advice you ever got about writing?" And more. Lots of articles and information for young writers, too. A friendly and supportive environment. Check it out.

The Inscription Project: A Look at Modern Writing

http://icse1.ucsd.edu/aasarava/

This fascinating website offers you insight into the history of writing. Most interesting feature: a timeline (click on History of Writing) that takes you from c. 20,000 B.C. ("Notches on animal bones used in Africa and elsewhere for record keeping—a prelude to writing in these regions.") through 1985 ("The computer becomes a common household item."). Coincidentally, every time my hard drive crashes, I use animal bones for my backup files—thereby bringing the history of writing full circle.

International Book Information Center

http://unc.edu/ibic./IBIC-homepage.html

This site provides a vast array of information about what's available to authors on the Internet. The brainchild of its editor and publisher, W. Frederick Zimmerman, IBIC has won praise for its clear, consistent, and well-organized approach to the task of bringing order to all the writing- and publishing-related resources on the Internet. *Publishers Weekly* calls it "the granddaddy" of all such websites. Booksellers, libraries, readers, rare books, international publishing, poetry, short stories, Web review databases—Zimmerman takes you through each topic with clarity, insight, and good humor. You'll also enjoy the Commonplace Book, which lists authors' comments on various subjects of importance to the human condition, such as Gandhi on cultures, Lincoln on bigotry, and Pirsig on hurrying. Even Pirsig, author of *Zen and the Art of Motorcycle Maintenance*, would advise you to hurry to this site.

Nonfiction Book Proposals

http://www.bookbuzz.com/sheree.htm

An excellent, concise summary of what goes into a nonfiction book proposal comes to us from the New York literary agency of Sheree Bykovsky. You'll also find a step-by-step guide to getting published, along with recommended books on publishing. This is the simplest, clearest guide to nonfiction book proposals—and to the publishing process in general—that I've seen on the Web. Or anywhere else, for that matter.

Of related interest: Agents

RECOMMENDED

Paradigm Online Writing Assistant

http://www.idbsu.edu/english/cguilfor/paradigm

An interactive, menu-driven, online writer's guide and handbook written by Chuck Guilford, an English professor at Boise State University who's been teaching people to write for 30 years.

How to write essays—informal, thesis/support, exploratory, or argumentative. Also beautifully written essays on discovering what to write, organizing your writing, revising your writing, editing, and how to document sources. Too bad this didn't exist when I was in school. A brief quote from "In Search of Form," one part of the essay on organizing your writing: "Everything that exists has a form. In writing, the goal is to find an appropriate form, one that suits your material and your purpose. Such a pattern may offer itself early in your writing process, or you may have to try out several possibilities before finding a suitable design. Either way, a strong organizational pattern helps both you and your reader." Gorgeous.

Publishing Scams

http://www.Webcube.com/authors/scams.htm

From the friendly folks at WebCube, an online bookstore and service provider for writers. This article explains that publishing scams fall into three groups: services to writers, including editing, organizations, and agenting; education for writers through correspondence schools; and publications, including "prizes." Learn who the bad guys are and how to protect yourself. A most useful essay.

Incidentally, this website is an excellent way for a consultant or other businessperson to promote himself or herself. Write an article about what you do, give lots of excellent information, and then let the reader know that you're available on a one-on-one basis. Now that's good marketing.

Publishing on a Shoestring

http://vanbc.wimsey.ca/~jhesse/

A short article about and guide to self-publishing. The author—who consults for other authors, as well as writing his own books—gives you the clear and concise information you need to produce, print, list, and sell your self-published book. The one thing that isn't in either piece is a warning about just how hard it is to self-publish. You're no longer just an author; you're a publishing company, and that's a big, expensive job. If you intend to publish on a shoestring, make sure the shoes to which they are attached are Bruno Magli or better—because you'll need lots of dollars to make the venture work. Remember that most small businesses that fail do so because of (1) lack of a business plan or (2) undercapitalization. In other words, don't finance yourself on your Visa card.

Text Archives

gopher://wiretap.Spies.COM/11/Etext

A melange, a potpourri: You make the call. Here you'll find a variety of text archives from universities around the country, including Skidmore, Mississippi State, and Michigan, as well as from other sites like the Interpedia, The Stacks, and the Library of Congress. This is interesting less as a research tool (there are many other, better-organized ones) and more as an illustration of where things are on the Internet right now. Everybody's trying to categorize all human knowledge, and it's just too big a job.

If you want a quick overview of what various folks are doing to make the Internet manageable, check this out. Otherwise, head directly to the site that most nearly meets your needs.

Writer's Resource Center

http://www.azstarnet.com/~poewar/writer/writer.html

John Hewitt's Web Page

AKA: PoeWar's Hideaway

Essays by John Hewitt, writer and poet, and essays by writers he likes, on subjects important to every writer: "Finding Time to Write"; "How to Become an Expert Writer in Any Field"; "Overcoming Writer's Isolation"; and so on. The article on isolation was of particular interest to me as I stared silently at the Web, reviewing sites for you. His reminders are quite useful: Remember that you have a radio. Join a gym. There's an outside to your house or apartment. Go visit it. Think I'll do that now.

Back Forward Home Reload Images Open Print Find Stop

CHAPTER TWELVE

PERSONAL FINANCE

You can use the Internet not just to make money as a writer but to learn how to spend it, invest it, and reduce your taxes as well. These sites provide vast quantities of information about every aspect of personal finance, from how to use your computer as a checkbook, to how to calculate the tax savings from buying a home, to how to evaluate and purchase any one of hundreds of mutual funds. Incidentally, here's how to get rich: take 10 percent of your gross income and stick it in any conservative investment vehicle, and leave it there. Give the next 10 percent to a charitable organization from which you currently derive some benefit (a religious institution, a 12 step program, whatever). Finally, quit going out to eat so often. It's that simple.

The Center For Debt Management

http://members.aol.com/DebtRelief/index.html

Too much month at the end of the money? The kind folks at the Family Debt Arbitration and Counseling Services, Inc. of Manchester and Candia, New Hampshire can help. They provide astonishing amounts of extremely well-organized information about how to get out of debt; how to change the way you handle money, credit cards, and government services; bankruptcy; how to avoid scams; and much more. Credit counseling and debt management services are available. The company charges a fee for its debt consolidation services but there is no fee to browse its comprehensive Internet archives.

Checkers, Simon, & Rosner

http://www.checkers-llp.com/

This Chicago-based accounting firm uses Internet technology to find new clients and to provide anyone interested with useful corporate and personal tax and business accounting information. This sort of marketing is absolutely the next wave of client development. Anyone interested in increasing their client base ought to take a look at what Checkers is up to already. You'll find an interesting article called "Sales Tax and the Internet" that is worthy of your attention, whatever your current field of business.

The Dollar Stretcher

http://www.stretcher.com/

This online version of Gary Foreman's syndicated column on family finance offers tips on subjects like home improvement; car care; banking; cleaning; appliances; Christmas; and dozens more. You'll find information on topics from gardening to garage sales to how to make the most of a college visit. You can also subscribe to a free e-mail newsletter simply by using their e-mail form. Most impressive and extremely useful.

RECOMMENDED

FinanCenter

http://www.financenter.com

Make better buying decisions for those big-ticket items: houses, cars, credit card loans. This intriguing website actually provides you with free extremely powerful calculators that let you make determinations such as, "Should I buy that house?" or "Should I refinance my loan?" An entirely Web-based business, it's free to you and it's paid for by finance companies and other financial service providers who benefit from leads that the site generates. Each section—Stocks, Bonds, Retirement Planning, Mutual Funds, Home, and Savings, to name a few—offers questions and answers on important topics for consumers and provides you with price quotes and other essential information. Click on **AutoCenter** and you'll get answers to questions like "Which is better—new or used?" and "How long should I keep a car?" You'll also find a glossary of auto loan terms and quotes for cars in your area.

Franklin Quest

http://franklinquest.com/

They say that no one's values, goals, or dreams ever make it onto their To Do list. How do you keep from getting swamped by the trivial? How do you keep track of the details, the Big Picture, your tax receipts, your goals, and your Aunt Martha's birthday? With a Franklin Day Planner, of course. Your author thinks the world of his Franklin Day Planner and uses it because he's far too intelligent to trust his mind to remember what time he's supposed to go to lunch. The website provides you with an overview of Franklin products and information about the seminars the company provides to help people use the planners. Franklin Quest recently merged with the Stephen Covey organization (he of *The Seven Habits of Highly Effective People* and the new *Seven Habits of Highly Effective Families*); you can learn about their joint efforts here, as well.

Kiplinger Online

http://Kiplinger.com

Millions of decision-makers and savvy investors have relied on Kiplinger's newsletters, books, and publications for decades. Now the cybernaut can, too. Here you'll find financial advice; forecasts; stock quotes; essays; and information you can use immediately to improve your financial life. You'll also find sample issues of "The Kiplinger Washington Letter" and "The Kiplinger Tax Letter" and excerpts from *Kiplinger's Personal Finance Magazine*. It's all presented in a lively, informative way. This is exactly what your parents want you to know about personal finance. Visit here anyway.

Money Magazine

http://pathfinder.com/money

Personal finance news, a constantly updated Business Report, and a thorough Marketwatch lead the list of features at this site. The most compelling reason to come back again and again is a search engine that allows you to type in a keyword, phrase or name and retrieve articles from all of Time-Life's publications including *Sports Illustrated*, *Time*, and *Fortune* magazines. I dare you to visit this site and not get side-tracked for hours or days. Incidentally, at the time of my visit, one *Money* magazine article explained that 60 percent of Americans think the tax code should be abolished—and 95 percent of those responding to an online survey thought the same thing. Well, I'd like to see the IRS abolished. I'd also like ice cream to be completely non-fattening and I'd like to have someone come over in about an hour and paint my house.

Quicken

RECOMMENDED

http://www.qfn.com/

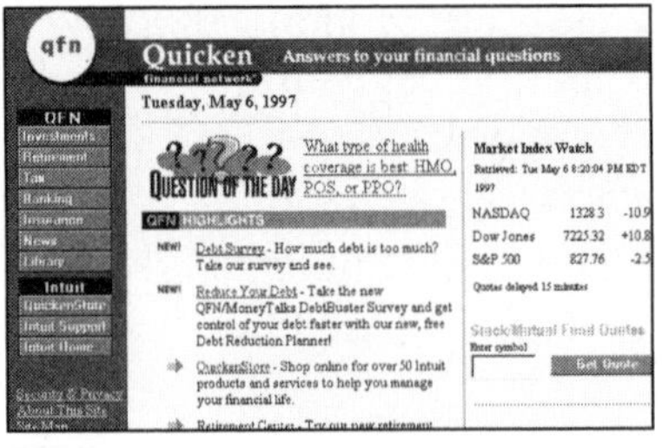

Intuit's Quicken is the leading software program for personal and business cash management. Write checks, manage your budget, keep your tax records . . . all on your personal computer. The website goes far beyond a sales pitch for the software and provides tons of valuable information on debt reduction, credit card rates, mutual funds, and thorny legal issues such as "Are there legal ramifications for paying household help 'under the table'?" Tax, retirement, insurance, and investment information as well. Deftly organized and extremely useful.

The Syndicate

http://www.moneypages.com/syndicate/index.html

One of the oldest, continuously operated investment related websites on the Internet, authored by a broker with serious Internet expertise. You'll find annotated links to hundreds of websites organized by topic: "Stocks"; "Bonds"; "Mutual Funds"; "Accounting and Taxes"; "The Dow 30 On The Web"; "Legal"; "Newsletters"; and many, many more. This is not a commercial site; it's simply a place where a highly knowledgeable individual has chosen for you the best websites related to investing and personal finance. I clicked on **Mutual Funds** and found links, with descriptions, to approximately 100 mutual fund companies and related enterprises. A "Bookstore" offers a list of recommended books that you can order directly from Amazon.com.

CHAPTER THIRTEEN

PROMOTION AND MARKETING

Many writers have the delusion that all they have to do is write a good book and the publisher will handle all the marketing chores. Wrong. The writer—not the house—is responsible for promoting and marketing the book. You can find many good books on marketing and promotion. It's just that most writers view themselves as artists who are somehow above the squalid world of self-promotion.

The Internet—specifically, the sites listed below—offers you two specific features when it comes to marketing. One is free, up-to-the-minute information, often provided by experts in publicity and marketing who are looking for authors like you to represent. The second is a brand-new way to market yourself as a writer.

Here is a simple, easy-to-follow Internet marketing plan that allows you to take full advantage of cyberspace for virtually no money.

STEP ONE Get a Web page. You can pay someone to design it or you can create it yourself. It's not that hard. Many newer word processors (Microsoft Word 97, for example) already include some basic tools. You can download several excellent HTML editors from the Internet (try the Tucows site: *http://www.tucows.com* or Shareware.com: *http://www.shareware.com*). Read Appendix C, "Website Creation."

On your Web page, describe yourself and your work. Provide excerpts and a photograph of yourself. Keep the Web page simple and short—if it's long, no one will have the patience to download it.

STEP TWO Become a marketing partner of Amazon.com or some other online bookstore. (See Chapter 8, "Booksellers Online.") As a marketing partner, you can link your Web page directly to Amazon, so that if a reader visits your website and wants to buy your book, you can have them click directly to Amazon.com and order it. It's convenient for the reader; you don't have to worry about fulfilling orders or taking people's Visa numbers; and on top of that, as a marketing partner of Amazon.com, you get eight percent of the purchase price. Pretty neat, huh?

STEP THREE Link your website with Yahoo!, Alta Vista, Magellan, Lycos, Excite, and every other leading search engine; to online reading forums; and to the lists of links you'll find in this book. Add yourself to all of the appropriate authors' lists mentioned in Chapter 2, "Authors," and link yourself to your publisher's home page. (See Chapter 3, "Publishing Houses," for a listing of websites that link virtually every publisher on the planet or search for your publisher by name in any major search engine.)

STEP FOUR Study the newsgroups and mailing lists mentioned in Appendix B, "Mailing Lists & Newsgroups." Determine which ones are amenable to receiving a brief and courteous message from you describing your new book and your website.

Before the recent explosion of interest in the Web, "netiquette" forbade commercial messages in websites. It was considered rude. Interestingly, the very people who made up rules about what is rude and what isn't were very happy to send dozens or even hundreds of angry, spiteful messages to those who violated their rules. Fortunately, those people have retreated, for the most part, to their caves, where they anxiously await getting a life. Still, be brief, courteous, and appropriate when you communicate a commercial message to newsgroups and mailing lists, because some of those rude beasts still walk the earth.

STEP FIVE Write your next book, or poem, or article, secure in the knowledge that Internet-goers around the globe have constant access to information about you and your works and that even as you work, play, and sleep, others are learning about you, buying your work, and benefiting from your literary achievements.

Sounds like fun, doesn't it? Herewith the best sites on the Internet to educate and assist you in developing your cybermarketing strategy.

Book and Candle Pub

http://www.cris.com/~Pubhost/webauthr.html

A special interest group on Delphi for the discussion of "books, authors, and everyday life." The focus of the site is on readers, not writers, but as an author you are welcome to offer yourself as a guest in their "Pub Forum." There you can take part in an online conference and also respond to a week's worth of forum notes from the participants. When last I visited, no big names had as yet taken advantage of this opportunity; here's a chance for you to get to know some serious readers.

Book Buzz—Facts About the Publishing Industry, and More

http://www.bookbuzz.com/

The home page of Susannah Greenberg Public Relations, a firm that represents authors and publishers. What makes this site so appealing is the information about the publishing industry it offers: reports by the Book Industry Study Group indicating the current situation and future of the book buying world. Americans will spend over $31 billion on books in the year 2000, up from $19 billion in 1990. Specifics and statistics on your industry, available for you here.

Also an extremely useful essay, "How to Get Your Book Published"—broken down into "What Happens First" and "What Happens Next"—offers a concise guide to the events that take you from idea to Oprah. This, along with a list of recommended books on the process of publishing and selling a book, and an excellent summary of what goes into a nonfiction book proposal, come to us from the New York literary agency of Sheree Bykovsky.

Of related interest: Agents

Book Marketing Online

RECOMMENDED

http://www.heritage.co.uk/heritage/hpr/book_marketing_online.html

This site is to help publishers and authors with cybermarketing, or selling books online. According to the site's authors, this includes creating websites for books or companies; cultivating relationships and mutual links with other websites; listing with search engines; posting in appropriate newsgroups; hosting author forums; and more. You'll find essays on how the major publishers like Penguin, Scholastic, and HarperCollins are marketing on the Net. You'll learn how to optimize your use of e-mail, which are the top search engines, how to use Usenet newsgroups, and much more. A quite useful site for anyone seeking to market online.

Books AtoZ

RECOMMENDED

http://www.booksatoz.com/

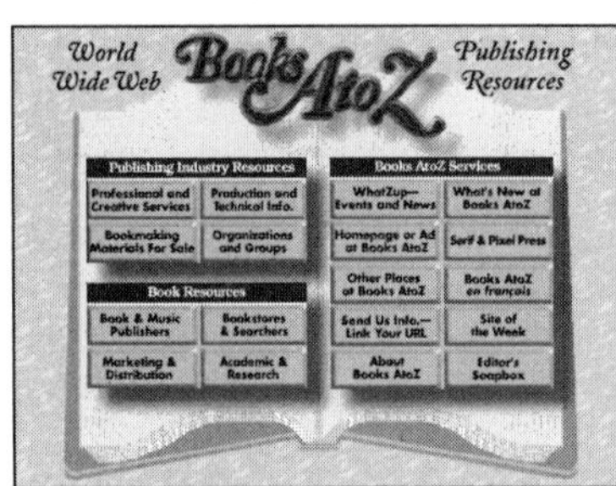

A monster website dedicated to helping people produce, distribute, and find books. This massive and excellent resource contains, among other things, lists of bookstores across the United States; a list of hundreds of professional organizations related to writing and publishing, some with links; a smaller list of publishing and writing organizations outside the United States; links to book designers, printers, computer services, and business and technical services for publishers; academic links, including chatbooks and monographs online; and tons more. My hat's off to these fine people, who make it truly easy to locate people to help you create and market your work.

RECOMMENDED

Booktalk

http://www.booktalk.com/

This fascinating website can teach authors a lot about writing, publishing, and marketing. Typical archived articles include a piece on costume reference books, providing "invaluable insight whether you are doing historicals or time travels"; how an author of vampire romances is marketing a line of sleepshirts and T-shirts featuring her main character, a "dangerously seductive vampire" named Valerian; a literary agent discussing how to write "attention-grabbing query letters with cover copy spin"; and an interview with the former president of Harlequin. With links to and information about beaucoup agents, publishers, authors, and much more. If you're not regularly visiting this site, you're missing a free education in how to succeed in publishing. An insider's website.

Canadian Publishers Council

http://www.pubcouncil.ca/

An excellent guide to getting published, or reprinted, in Canada. Links to and information about virtually everything happening in Canadian publishing. A FAQ, a list of frequently asked questions, is of particular use to first-time authors in or out of Canada and to those who seek employment in publishing. Essays and reports on the state of the written word in Canada round out this most useful site.

Coyote: A Literary Arts Foundation for the West

http://www.coyote-arts.org/

If you have a literary arts organization and you want to get on the Internet, Coyote can help you. They also publish *Bakunin*, an annual journal of avant-garde literature and art. The website itself hasn't got much to look at; it's apparently just a way of letting arts groups know that they can get on the Internet through them.

C-Span Booknotes

gopher://c-span.org:70/00/Schedule/Booknotes

Weekly hour-long interviews with leading authors and author/news-makers. You can find a master list of all the shows and order copies of the interviews via this Gopher menu. It would be so nice if excerpts from some of those interviews could be found here as well. The archive was about six months behind when last I visited.

Gebbie Press

http://www.gebbieinc.com

Here you will find e-mail addresses, with links that let you send e-mail directly via the Web, for newspapers and radio and television stations across the United States, organized alphabetically by state. An extremely useful tool for authors who want to promote themselves without incurring vast expenses for postage and photocopying—not to mention how much time can be saved. A service of Gebbie Press, brainchild of Mark Gebbie. Gebbie Press specializes in promotion on the Web.

Internet Marketing—FSB Associates Home Page

http://www.fsbassociates.com/

This Internet marketing company can help fashion an online publicity campaign using a website, mailing lists, newsgroups, and online bookstores. The site is useful as an introduction to the marketing possibilities of the Net, offering clear and straightforward descriptions of how to use the various components of the Net to sell your book. You can also read a chapter of Phaedra Hise's online book, "Growing Your Business Online."

Marketing Experts and Literary Agents

http://www.bookwire.com/index/Publicity-and-Marketing.html

Here you will find hyperlinks to dozens of book marketing firms and literary agencies with presences on the Internet. I've listed a few in this book, concentrating on those whose Web pages have information useful to all writers. You can scroll through these sites and see whether you'd like to do business with these friendly and Internet-savvy folks.

Of related interest: Agents

RECOMMENDED

Midwest Book Review

http://www.execpc.com/~mbr/bookwatch/

The Midwest Book Review was founded in 1980 and produces "Bookwatch," a weekly television program reviewing books, videos, music, and new technology for 86,000 households on a Madison, Wisconsin, cable TV system. It also publishes library newsletters and posts all its reviews with America Online. Publishers can offer their books for review on the site; individuals can learn how to become book reviewers for the Midwest Book Review. A

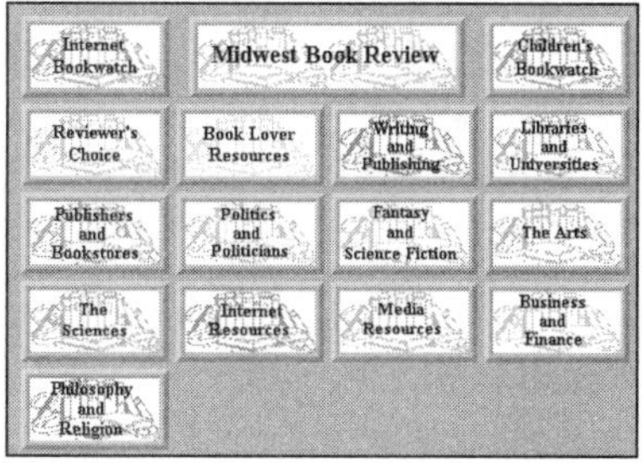

key feature: annotated links to Web pages covering hundreds of subjects of interest to writers, organized by topics like "Politics and Politicians," the "Sciences," "Business and Finance," and "Philosophy and Religion." The "Internet Bookwatch" section offers reviews of hundreds of titles, many from small or academic presses, arranged by more subjects than I've seen anywhere else on the Web. A very impressive site.

My Memories Publishing

http://www.mymemories.com/

An intriguing website. This company, located in Capistrano Beach, California, believes that everyone has a story to tell and that your memories can be instructive for others. To that end, they offer you a place to sell your book to readers. Most of the authors whose work is available via My Memories Publishing sell their books either as hard copies or via 3.5" floppy disks for around $10. Fiction and nonfiction works are available; topics include everything from divorce and death to "torrid island romance."

My Memories, whose majordomo is 75 years old, sticks up for the "little guy and gal"—the people whose books aren't right for the major publishing houses because sales would be too small. You can find out how to list your books with My Memories and you can order the works of other authors via e-mail at the site.

National Media Services

http://www.jaxnet.com/~media-pr/

One-stop shopping for authors in need of a publicist. National Media Services provides online and traditional promotion for authors and publishing houses. They also publish books but stress that they are not a vanity press. Their Web page includes a helpful article explaining why authors need publicists (and they usually do). They also provide links to a decent number of authors, publishers, and resources for writers.

RECOMMENDED

Publishers Marketing Association Online

http://pma-online.org/pmahome.html

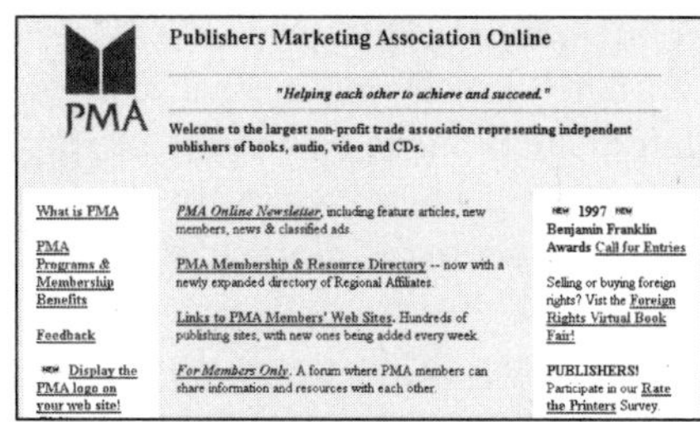

PMA is the independent or small publisher's best friend and serves book, audio, and video publishers in the United States and around the world. The PMA online newsletter offers selected articles from the current issue and changes as often as weekly. Feature articles at the time of my visit included "Foreign Publishing Deals, Part II"; "Observations on Successful Publishing: Controlling Your Own Destiny"; "How to Create a Winning Direct Mail Package"; and "A Low Cost System For Marketing Novels Is Not a Work of Fiction." You'll also learn about marketing programs sponsored by PMA, including their "Foreign Rights Virtual Book Fair," which lets you buy and sell foreign rights to works in dozens of categories from Animals to Writing/Publishing. PMA is essential for a small or independent publisher's success; their excellent Web page shows you why.

Publishing on the Web

http://www.pubcouncil.ca/webguide.html

Say you want to start a publishing company on the World Wide Web. Go directly to the Canadian Publishing Council's bookmark of websites for their seminar for production and editorial managers, "Publishing on the Web," and you'll get all the answers. You'll find guidelines on how to choose an Internet service provider (with links to several dozen companies); directions on how to do a name search for and register the name of your new website; demographics and other marketing information related to the Net; suggestions for developing Web content; tools, databases, development guides . . . get the drift? It's complete, it's full of links, it's from Canada—what could be better?

Reader's Index

http://www.readersndex.com/

I'm puzzled by this site. I can't quite figure out what it's for. It appears to be a fairly friendly commercial vehicle allowing publishers to provide readers information about new books. A special feature allows you to view a title and cover of a new book every 40 seconds; if you're interested, you can click on it and get more information. But in the history of the Internet, has anyone waited 40 seconds for anything? Also, you can't do the Auto-Browse by category, and the first titles that came up for me were novels for adolescents. A good idea that perhaps could use a bit of fine-tuning.

"Using E-Mail to Sell Your Writing"

ftp://rtfm.mit.edu/pub/usenet/news.answers./writing/resources/part1/

This essay sets forth a large number of outlets, both print and Internet, that purchase writing sent to them via e-mail. You'll find out what the publications are, how to reach them, whether and how much they pay, and what they're looking for. A companion essay (same URL but enter **part2/** at the end) is a letter to editors explaining why they should get with e-mail if they haven't done so already.

Yahoo! Books List

http://www.yahoo.com/Business/Corporations/Books

Hundreds of categories and subcategories listing thousands of books; you can look up books in every category, from Adult to Used and Rare. This is an excellent place to list your own book—why not have people plugging into Yahoo! find—and buy—*your* book?

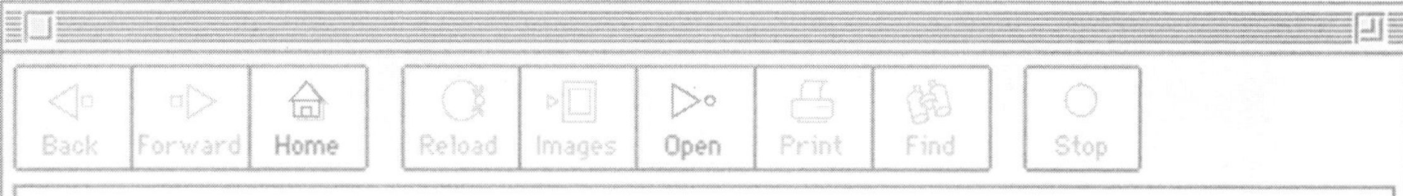

CHAPTER FOURTEEN

REVIEW SOURCES

These sites offer you places to find new books to read . . . or if you are marketing your own work, you'll find places where you should send your books for review. No one knows exactly how many people you can reach through these online review sources. Why pass up potential readers and sales?

Booklist

http://www.ala.org/booklist/

This website is meant to introduce new readers to *Booklist,* one of the leading pre-publication book review journals and one upon which booksellers and librarians rely heavily when choosing titles. The site offers reviews of books for adults; books for youth; audiovisual media; reference materials; and also provides an Editors' Choice list; lists of Best Books; and Feature Articles and Bibliographies. Special features include reviews of novels from Christian publishers, books in Spanish published in the U.S., and "Evaluating Encyclopedias—How We Do It." A vital resource for writers who want to learn more about what succeeds and why.

BookPage—Your Guide to the Best in New Books

http://www.bookpage.com/

BookPage "is a national review publication helping nearly one million people each month select their books and learn more about the people writing them." Reviews and interviews; a cover story on a current author; a place to post your own reviews; a searchable archive offering the last ten issues of BookPage; you'll also find an Advance Title list; and a bulletin board for "writers, publishers, and booklovers."

BookBrowser

http://www.PolyWeb.com/BookBrowser

Looking for something good to read? This remarkable site offers lists of good books by genre, by author, by time and place, and by age group. Click on the kind of book you want and you'll be rewarded with links to lists of great books in that field, award winners, and recommended titles from a variety of sources. Sponsored by Powell's Books of Oregon. You'll never again have to wonder what to read. And what you find you can immediately order from Powell's.

Bookplex

http://www.gigaplex.com/books/index.html

This new online superstore offers interviews, articles and excerpts by and about authors of new books. Popular culture is stressed here; the interviewee at the time of my visit was super-groupie Pamela Des Barres. Typical articles: a review of a history of punk rock and an essay on how to be "irresistible" to the opposite sex. With links to various lifestyle enhancements like yoga, sex, and film.

Bookwire's Computer Book Review

http://www.bookwire.com/cbr

Hundreds of reviews of new computer books for computer professionals, divided into fifteen categories, including: "Business Software"; "DBMS"; "Graphics"; "Hardware"; "Internet"; "Multimedia"; "Programming"; "Technology Management"; and "World Wide Web." An excellent feature: annotated lists of computer book publishers and computer bookstores, with links to same. You'll also find a link to Publishers Weekly's computer book bestsellers lists.

Chapter One

http://www.washingtonpost.com/wp-srv/style/longterm/books/books.htm

This intriguing feature of the Washington Post offers you the entire first chapters of new fiction and nonfiction books. The emphasis here is on thought-provoking books for intelligent readers; no potboilers or sex-filled bestsellers here. Every week the editors of the *Washington Post Book World* add three to seven first chapters. Politics and public policy are typical topics—

this *is* Washington—but you'll find a wide range of fascinating new works. During the week of my visit, the newly listed books included a biography of Edgar Allen Poe and a work by retired Senator Alan Simpson.

A Closer Look

http://www.acloserlook.com/

A Closer Look, offering "news and reviews of the latest in Christian Books, Music, and More." The "Inspired Choices" section gives readers reviews of best-loved new books; and reviews in categories like Children's Books; Christian Living; Devotionals; Family and Parenting; and Fiction. A bestsellers list and articles about new authors and books rounds out the site.

Electronic Review of Computer Books

http://www.ercb.com/

The Electronic Review of Computer Books has a modest desire: to be the equivalent of the New York Review of Books for books about computers. And I say, that's excellent. Always aim high. Here you'll find reviews of "awfully significant or significantly awful" new computer books; an archive of book reviews searchable by author or title; classifieds; letters; and long lists of newly received books. The technically minded will especially enjoy the reviews at this site.

Homespun: Favorite Reviews from Real Folks

http://www.best.com/~yylee/homespun/index.html

This website serves the book-reading public by providing you a place to post a list of your favorite books. You can also browse through the lists provided by hundreds of "real folks" like Winona's "The Books to Die For," Fanoula's "Don't tell me you haven't read these!" and Jordan's "Doctor's Off Call Reading." Eleanor Cohen thoughtfully offers "groovy reads with one word titles," including Possession, Bliss, Libra, Immortality and Lolita.

With e-mail links to the listmakers; perhaps you can strike up a friendship or kindle a romance with someone who shares your literary tastes. Great fun.

RECOMMENDED

New York Times Book Review

http://www.nytimes.com/books

An outstanding site. Here you'll find the latest *New York Times* book reviews, bestseller lists, articles, features, author interviews, and an archive, searchable by author or title, of thousands upon thousands of book reviews from the daily and Sunday *New York Times*. The Internet at its best—a wonderfully useful tool for anyone who loves books. Membership in the *New York Times* online is required; it's free and easy to receive.

Smartbooks

http://www.smartbooks.com/

Paradox underlies the mission of this excellent website dedicated to books about the Internet: its creators view the Internet as the world's greatest source of information. But if you want to learn about the Internet, they suggest, and discover where to find all that wonderful information, you're better off reading books than searching the Web. This site organizes and reviews countless books about the Internet, dividing them into dozens of topics like "Programming"; "Languages"; "Intranets"; "Internet Marketing"; and "Commerce on the Web." With links to bookstores that allow you to order the books over the Web. You can sign up for weekly updates and check out the Book of the Week; Author of the Month; Publisher of the Month; and many other features.

Yahoo Book Review Sites

http://www.yahoo.com/text/Arts/Humanities/Literature/Books/Reviews

This list features links to dozens of book review sites, large and small, personal and professional, from around the world. You can search it by Children's Books; Nonfiction; Recommended Reading Lists; or Science

Fiction, Fantasy, and Horror. Listed reviewers include Chuck, Ed, Danny Yee, Jenny and John, as well as the Christian Fiction Review, Native American Books, and the Romance Reader.

Yahoo Recommended Newsgroups

http://www.yahoo.com/Arts/Humanities/Books_and_Literature/Usenet/

Here you'll find nine (at last count) newsgroups, recommended by Yahoo, offering commentary, reviews, and press releases related to business, technical, computer, and general interest books. Yahoo recommends these newsgroups presumably because they're popular and (relatively) free of purely commercial messages ("Make A Million Dollars With Your Computer!"). I don't think too highly of these newsgroups simply because there's no quality control. Anybody can post anything about anything; you can spend a lot of time digging through these sites and learn nothing. You might have unlimited Internet access but you don't have unlimited time. Spend it wisely; spend it elsewhere.

CHAPTER FIFTEEN

YOUNG ADULT, MIDDLE GRADE, AND CHILDREN'S WRITING

Here you will find excellent resources for writing for young people of all ages. You'll find sites for kids, teens, adults, librarians (not that librarians aren't adults; you know what I mean), booksellers, and everyone else. These sites offer lists of recommended books, places for young people to post their work, and tons of information for authors seeking to publish books for young readers.

Books for Children and More—an Editor's Site **RECOMMENDED**

http://www.users.interport.net/~hdu/

If you write for children or young adults or you're even thinking about doing so, start right here. Harold C. Underdown is a leading editor of children's books, and he maintains a gloriously useful site for authors in the field. You'll find excellent essays on how to get published; how to avoid the "slush pile" (publisher's slang for unsolicited manuscripts); what to avoid doing; what sells; what doesn't; and other forms of great advice. Among the suggestions: don't try to rhyme like Dr. Seuss—most people can't do it. Avoid strange or alliterative character names like "Harry the Horizon Line."

Don't concentrate on creating a series right away—just work on *a good manuscript.* He also suggests that you click on his lists of award-winning children's books and read them. Links to other children's book websites here, too. A great site.

Bookwire—Publishing for Young Readers

http://www.bookwire.com/index/Publishing-for-Young-Rdrs.html

Drop in if you're interested in publishing for young readers and you want to see what resources the Internet has to offer. Annotated links to dozens of intriguing sites; everything from African literature for young readers to the Young Writers Club. Commercial and nonprofit sites. An excellent way to quickly find the key sites for young readers, the authors who write for them, and their publishers.

Canadian Teacher-Librarian's Resource Page **RECOMMENDED**

http://www.inforamp.net/~abrown/

Several hundred annotated links to everything under the children's literature sun: associations, authors and illustrators, awards, book lists, journals and magazines, newsgroups and listservs, public libraries, publishers, reviews, school libraries, titles and series, and dozens more links. Awesome.

Of related interest: Lists of Links

RECOMMENDED

Children's Writing Resource Center

http://www.mindspring.com/~cbi/index.html

A product of *Children's Book Insider,* a newsletter for children's writers and illustrators. The CBI is the official and exclusive update source for the *Children's Writers & Illustrators Market,* published by Writer's Digest.

The InfoCenter offers a FAQ covering "Writing For Children"; a list of "Commonly Used Publishing Terms & Phrases"; "Characters"; "Humor"; "Pivotal Points of Fiction"; "Special Reports"; and much more. The FAQ does an excellent job of answering the questions of those new to the field, and you'll find highlights from the current month's CBI as well as the "Hot Market Tip of the Month." This month's tip is a pretty good one: the *Cricket Magazine* group, in conjunction with *Smithsonian* magazine, will launch a nonfiction magazine for children aged 6–14. How to reach them and what they buy—find it here.

Cinderella and Little Red Riding Hood Project

http://www-dept.usm.edu/~engdept/lrrh/lrrhhome.htm

The nightmare of every parent whose child is an English major: close textual study of fairy tales. Yes, but how are you going to get a job? Here you will find a dozen textual versions of Cinderella, dating from the 18th through 20th centuries, and 16 versions of Little Red Riding Hood.

Cyber-Girl

http:www.angelfire.com/pg0/GIRL/index.html

An online magazine just for teen girls. Comes with this warning: "Everyone, I'm sorry, but I'm very busy and don't have the time to keep up with the magazine. Between school, 4-H, homework, my boyfriend, and modeling I just can't seem to find the time!" Always does a lot for my ego to find a 13-year old with more of a life than I have. Actually, if you write for teens, it makes a lot of sense to get to know sites like this. Meet your readers where they are—online, reading magazines like this one. You'll find more such links at the Young Adult Librarian's Help/Home Page, reviewed in Chapter 33, "Librarians' Resources."

de Grummond Children's Literature Collection

http://www.lib.usm.edu/degrumm.htm

One of the leading collections of children's literature in North America, the de Grummond collection contains original manuscripts, artworks, and books. It's located at the University of Southern Mississippi and will handle reference questions by mail, telephone, and e-mail. The website is attractive, growing rapidly, and an excellent introduction to the study of children's literature. See also the Childrens Book Festival, listed in Chapter 7, "Book Fairs." You can view only a small number of the thousands of items in the collection, but they are quite lovely, such as a hat created by children's book author and illustrator Ezra Jack Keats at *http://ocean.st.usm.edu/~dajones/images/jenhat.gif*

Of related interest: Librarians' Resources

Inkspot

http://www.interlog.com/~ohi/inkspot/

This attractive and bountiful site offers market information, classifieds, forums, articles, FAQs, genres, and a writing workshop for writers of all fields and at all levels. We've culled some of the especially useful Inkspot features and placed them in various categories throughout this book. "Market Information" provides annotated links to dozens of publishers and lets you know what they're looking for. "Classifieds" list authors in search of publishers; publishers in search of authors; agents; screenplays; and much more. You can find some serious opportunities in amongst the silly (a Spanish author named Cervantes seeks a publisher for a book called Don Quixote; a screenwriter offers his "Pulp Fiction-ish" screenplay for $500). You can also get a free subscription to *Inklings*, a biweekly newsletter containing the highlights of the website. Also a list of "Associations For Writers" . . . and more than can be jammed into one of our entries. Do visit.

Internet Public Library—Youth and Teens

http://ipl.sils.umich.edu/

This excellent service from the University of Michigan is part of a real-live library online; students should definitely visit the Reference section so that they can lift entire portions of scholarly works and paste them verbatim into their school essays. Just kidding. Kids will find here a writing contest; "Ask the Author"; "Story Hour"; book reviews by kids for kids; and "Dr. Internet," who explores math and science, fun and facts. Teens will find sections on arts and entertainment; books and writing; career and college (they do things in pairs in Ann Arbor, notice that?); clubs and organizations; school topics; and sports. For example, the "Books and Writing" section offers author information, book lists, and writing instruction. I clicked on **Writing instruction** because reviewers are always suggesting I get some, and I found links to writing groups and organizations for young adults. An attractive and safe place for kids of all ages. For more information on the reference department of this website, see Chapter 33, "Libraries Online."

Kidpub

http://www.kidpub.org/kidpub/

This popular site (over 2,000,000 visitors served) began because a father wanted to encourage his 9-year-old daughter to write. Now, kids and entire schools post stories on this site. Your child can read the stories and post stories of his or her own. Most intriguing story title: "HELP! I'M A PRISONER ON THE INTERNET!" by Ashley S., age 9, of Ohio. Hey, Ashley, since I've been working on this book I know exactly how you feel. She writes: "I love the Internet, but my father says I misuse it. I type in 10 commands for the computer before it completes the task it's currently doing. What's so bad about that? Computers are supposed to work fast. Don't you agree? Don't you?"

Kidsweb

http://www.npac.syr.edu/textbook/kidsweb/literature.html

Annotated links to young reader-friendly websites related to literature. You'll find "The Wrath of the Bard—Shakespearean Insults"; lots of online children's stories; fairy tales and fables; poetry; the complete works of

William Shakespeare; stories and writings of indigenous peoples; science fiction; and some more stuff on Shakespeare. Seriously, this is a thoughtful and well-chosen list of links that might even distract adolescent boys from Pamela Anderson Web pages. Okay, so I'm dreaming. But it's definitely worth a visit. A service of the kind folks at Syracuse University.

Quill Society

http://www.quill.net/

The Quill Society offers 12- to 24-year-old writers a place to publish their work online. The club's founders say they created the website out of a sense of frustration that their work wasn't taken seriously because they are young writers. You can join Quill and your stories will appear in the appropriate section: adventure, sci fi, mystery, fiction, poetry, bestsellers, or periodicals. You can also have your work evaluated by a Board of Critics; if that's not enough pain for you, I can give you my family's e-mail addresses and they'll evaluate your whole life. Seriously, the level of the writing was remarkably high for writers of any age, and this site deserves high marks. There's also an online member chatroom that meets once a week; you can meet like-minded writers your age and have fun.

CHAPTER SIXTEEN

DRAMA AND PLAYWRITING

This part of the Writers' Internet serves as a vast home for playwrights, actors, producers, and theatergoers. Here you can find places to publish your plays online so that producers or others can read them and gain interest in you. You can read plays from Aristophanes to modern times. You can read about plays, about theaters and theater companies, and about playwrighting workshops. The section concludes with a brief list of Usenet Newsgroups of interest to the theater-minded.

Brief Guide to Internet Resources in Theater and Performance Studies

http://www.stetson.edu/~csata/thr_guid.html

By Ken McCoy, theater and Internet expert. Here you'll find carefully chosen and well-described links to everything theater-related that's of interest to a broad spectrum of people. McCoy explains that he's not trying to create a compendium of every theater-related website, just those of most use to cybersurfers interested in the study of the theater. Topics include "Most Helpful Sites"; "Actors and Acting"; "Stagecraft and Technical Theater"; "Plays and Playwrights"; "Shakespeare"; and much, much more. **Plays and Playwrights** brings you a list of places to publish your scripts on the Net, read articles about playwrighting, and find guides to and groups interested in writing for the theater.

By the way, have I shared with you my secret for getting really excellent service in restaurants in New York and L.A.? I wait until the waiter or waitress is hovering over me. I keep my face buried in the menu and then say with a dark scowl, "I don't even know why I went INTO casting."

Works like a charm.

Children's Theater Resource Webpage

http://pubweb.acns.nwu.edu/~vjs291/children.html

For adults, about children's theater. This site offers state-by-state listings of children's theaters, with information on internships and more. There are links to associations and groups dedicated to children's theater, and home pages for websites about children's theater. You'll find children's literature resources, and a history of children's theater and biographies of leading figures in this branch of stagecraft.

Drama Collection

http://english-www.hss.cmu.edu/drama/

Part of the English Server at Carnegie-Mellon University, this site includes plays, screenplays, and discussions of drama and dramatic productions. Titles currently available include 11 comedies by Aristophanes, John Gay's *The Beggar's Opera*; Goethe's *Faust*; the plays of Ben Jonson; lyrics to a variety of Broadway plays of the 1970s and 1980s—and all the lyrics to four Gilbert and Sullivan operas. One questions the copyright legitimacy of those song lyrics.

Writers who love the Internet because it delivers anything they want to their computer should take note of the fact that, until 15 years ago, there was a large and thriving business in this country in sheet music. Lyricists were compensated for their efforts. Writers should be aware of the problem that the Internet poses for us—it is the world's largest copying machine: Once your work is posted, anyone can read it and you won't get a penny in royalties. Something to think about.

You can go directly to Gilbert and Sullivan by typing in *gopher://gopher.etext.org:70/00/Quartz/theater/musicals/GilbertSullivan/*

Dramatic Exchange

http://www.dramex.org/

Light the cyberlights: Here is a place where playwrights can publish and distribute their plays, where producers can find new plays to produce, and where anyone else can read new drama. Playwrights on all levels are welcome. Plays are indexed alphabetically, by type (comedy, tragedy, drama, mystery), by length (one act, full length, musical, screenplay), and also whether they involve audience participation or are considered "experimental."

I wanted to find a play at random, and I did: "Earwig," by Fraser MacFarlane. Three postal employees working at a dead-letter office discover a head in one of the packages they open. An argument ensues over what to do with it. Sigh. Once again, the Internet may have been turned into a great big invisible file cabinet for the unproduceable along with the unpublishable. If you are a playwright and sincerely want to have your work produced, you've got to question whether "publishing" it on the Internet really gets it before decision-makers. If the theatrical world is anything like book publishing, it's highly unlikely that a busy producer who has the power to say yes to a playwright would be looking for plays on a website. Not to throw cold water on a very good idea; just to suggest that the Internet isn't yet a substitute for doing whatever playwrights have to do to get their work read.

Essays on the Craft of Dramatic Writing

RECOMMENDED

http://www.teleport.com/~bjscript/index.htm

For writers of fiction, theater, and screenplays. This site gets the highest recommendation I can give: I wish I wrote it. You'll find thought-provoking, accurate, and exciting essays on topics like "Understanding What a Story Is"; "Foundation Principles of Storytelling"; "Understanding the Process of Storytelling"; "Anatomy of a Plot"; and much more. The author of the essays is Bill Johnson, and my writing hat is off to him. A superlative job, and a great use of the Internet. Run, don't walk—and let Johnson's ideas work their magic for you. This site offers recommended books, including excellent explanations of what you'll get out of those books.

Of related interest: Essays on Writing and Publishing

New Dramatists

http://www.itp.tsoa.nyu.edu/~diana/ndintro.html

New Dramatists, a leading playwrights' organization since its inception in 1949, chooses six playwrights a year for membership and offers all playwrights assistance and information through its website. A BBS, called "The Callboard," is open to anyone wishing to exchange "ideas, problems, discoveries, and/or inspirations on the art, craft, and livelihood of playwrighting." Threads include "Looking for plays!"; "Theaters looking for new works!"; "Format: How do you submit a script?"; and "Composers, book-writers, and lyricists." You'll also find a schedule of readings of members' plays; a photo gallery; applications for various playwrighting fellowships; a list of agents; an e-mail directory; and links to other theater-related sites.

Playwrighting Seminars

RECOMMENDED

http://www.vcu.edu/artweb/playwriting/seminar.html

Richard Toscan of the Virginia Commonwealth University School of the Arts has provided for you, free of charge, a 198-page guide to playwrighting. Toscan writes that America's 250 regional theaters (hyperlinks to many of them available here) have become the "research and development arm" of the commercial theater, and he focuses his comments on the writing of plays for regional playhouses. You'll learn about characters, conflict, settings, subjects, subtext, themes, titles, and many other subjects. You get examples of how plays should look; information on issues of structure like monologues, shape, style, time; and lots of fun quotes about playwrighting and the theater. An excellent site.

Playwright's Project

http://www.vnet.net/users/phisto/apphome.html

The idea of this site is to help writers as they start writing their plays, not when they're in their umpteenth rewrite. Three times a year, three-month sessions commence, involving around 10 writers along with a company of actors, directors, and other professionals. Those actors and directors will work with the playwrights from the beginning of the writing process so that the playwrights can visualize just how scenes will appear on stage. The Playwright's Project is located in North Carolina. You can become a part of it, or learn how to establish a similar project in your area, by dropping in here.

Theatre Central

http://www.theatre-central.com/

Don't forget to spell *theatre* their way as you point your browser to this award-winning site for playwrights and others interested in stagecraft. The site is a directory of theater resources on the Net, with links to general professional theater companies of all levels; specialty theater companies like Shakespeare, children's, young people's, and improv; listings of current theaters across the country; playwrights, composers, directors, actors, producers, and designers online; stagecraft; literature; and much more. I went to the summer stock link and found further links to six summer stock companies offering schedules, ticket information, and special events. A vast reference for theater folk.

Usenet Newsgroups for Theatre People

All the Internet's a stage, but these are the places where the play's the thing. My usual caveat about newsgroups applies here. People who are really serious about their artistic endeavors spend only a limited amount of time in newsgroups and recognize that newsgroups are usually more for the fun of it than for serious work. Enjoy yourself but don't mistake keeping busy for getting things done.

rec.arts.theatre.plays	Brief discussions of various plays
rec.arts.theatre.musicals	Discussions of favorite musicals and artists, such as Mandy Patinkin
rec.arts.theatre.stagecraft	Questions about staging, employment opportunities, workshops
rec.arts.theatre.misc	Q&A, the Globe theatre, information for actors
rec.arts.puppetry	Information on a degree in puppetry from the University of Connecticut, insults aimed at puppeteers
alt.stagecraft	How to stage scenes

CHAPTER SEVENTEEN

JOURNALISM RESOURCES

Journalists and those who love journalism will be delighted with these sites, which I have divided into two sections. The first helps you find experts in practically every field you can imagine—banking, law, politics, personal finance, modeling, traffic safety, even chocolate—and hundreds of other fields.

The second section takes you to archives and news sources from every conceivable news outlet on every continent. You'll also find fascinating essays on journalism . . . and some help with statistics, if you're about as much of a math genius as I am.

FINDING EXPERTS VIA THE INTERNET

Ask the Expert

http://www.pitsco.inter.net/askanexpert

This site offers you a list of topics and hooks you up, via e-mail, to experts in each of more than 100 fields. For example, "Ask a Banker" takes you to a website sponsored by the Oklahoma Bankers Association, which invites you to ask a question or offer a comment. You simply click where it says **Click here**, and you get an e-mail form with plenty of room for your question. I asked a question about mortgage loans. "Ask a Bird Expert" reminds you that "This is not to take the place of your vet." You can also reach experts in these fields: the census, cigars, geology, gravity, law, magic, models, mustangs . . . a wonderful source of information for every kind of writer.

Business Consultants and Experts

http://www.expertcenter.com/

Here you will find consultants and speakers on business-related aspects of sales, motivation, humor, diversity, leadership, and more. Includes biographies and photos of the speakers plus their topics, c.v.'s, recommendations, and downloadable articles they've written. You can benefit either from the articles or from contacting them directly with your questions. For example, I clicked on **Suzanne Vaughan** and learned that she is a motivational speaker whose theme is "The Stars Are Within You!" I can either download her article "Stress for Success: Coping and Thriving in the 90s" or I can reach her by mail, phone, fax, or e-mail.

RECOMMENDED

Counsel Quote

http://www.counsel.com/counselquote/

Need a quote from a lawyer for your story? Turn to this site and you'll find quotable quotes from top attorneys and law professors across the United States. Some of these people haven't exactly mastered the art of the soundbite, and they can be extremely wordy. But others have a knack for putting things simply and clearly. You can use this fascinating service in a number of ways—you can check the "Hot Topics" section and get quotes about current events. (At the time of my visit, gay marriages in Hawaii took center stage.) Or, you can post a query of your own, like "I'm looking for a lawyer who can discuss discrimination from a defense perspective." Why do lawyers do this? They're in business, and it's good public relations to be quoted in the media.

Other uses: check the listing of experts by specialty in "Experts On Call." You can poll lawyers about a particular issue with "Counsel Canvass." You can also turn to "Story Ideas," where attorneys "present you with topics they think may be exciting." I used the Counsel Canvass to ask, "Is the Internet the death of copyright?" I told them I was a nonfiction author and novelist and said that my deadline was six weeks from now, all of which is true. I'll let you know what results I get.

This is a fantastic use of the Internet and a real win-win situation: You get quotes, lawyers get quoted as experts. Excellent.

Of related interest: Law

RECOMMENDED

E-mail: MEDIA

http://www.ping.at/gugerell/media/

Any journalist, any nonfiction writer, any freelancer, any fiction writer, any human being who has to do research on any topic will do cartwheels and backflips over this stunning site. Literally thousands of e-mail addresses for individuals and organizations across the globe to speed your research work. A truly heroic job by one Peter Gugerell of Vienna, Austria. Typical listings include not just, say, the e-mail address of the *Boston Globe*, but e-mail addresses for its 15 different departments. You'll also find e-mail addresses for organizations as diverse as *Car and Driver, Computer Life, Late Night with David Letterman* (look under CBS), and thousands of other addresses. Mindblowing. Do not pass go; proceed directly to this site and be amazed.

Expert Rolodex

RECOMMENDED

gopher://gopher.igc.apc.org:70/11/orgs/alternet/expert

For media professionals only: alternative voices to mainstream political and social commentators. This excellent site gives you brief biographies and means of contacting several hundred "experienced, intellectually grounded, media-savvy experts who are available via a quick phone call, fax, or e-mail message." You can browse or search the "Expert Rolodex" by topic: For example, typing in "environment" yields 16 experts in environmental policy. Sample workplaces of the experts: Natural Resources Defense Council; Gay & Lesbian Alliance Against Defamation; Women in Prison Project; Interfaith Coalition for Immigrant Rights.

Experts—The Noble Internet Directory

http://WWW.experts.com

A global, online, interactive directory offering access to thousands of experts, spokespersons, and consultants in all fields. You type in the subject and, if you like, a location or ZIP code, and the service responds with a long list of experts, their specialties, and, if they have them, e-mail or Web addresses. Designed primarily for journalists and attorneys. I tried sports, personal finance, and traffic safety and found lots of experts in each category. Chocolate and orchestras turned up one each, whereas roses, daffodils, and insomnia turned up none. Chances are, if you've got a subject that could be contested in court, you're more likely to find experts here.

RECOMMENDED

National Press Club Directory of News Sources

http://www.access.digex.net/~npc/

Go where the big boys and girls go to get news. "A journalist's tip-of-the-fingers guide to expertise." And then some. Whatever your field, whatever your topic, whatever your genre, this list of excellent, well-chosen links to the best people and organizations in every field—all standing by to help you with your writing—is a must.

Topics include addictions counseling, adoption, advertising/public relations, county government, health care (a vast resource itself), higher education, and dozens of other topics with hundreds and hundreds of links.

NEWS OUTLETS, ARCHIVES, AND ESSAYS

The African Writer's Series D Africa Online

http://www.africaonline.com/AfricaOnline/griotstalk/writers/series/jj.html

A brief listing of African authors with titles, book descriptions, and some links to their publishers. I wish there were more to report—like excerpts, or links to biographies or Web pages, or anything else, but that's all there is at this site right now. Find links to the African Newsstand, which provides ten Africa news sources in English and other languages.

Of related interest: Black and Hispanic Resources

RECOMMENDED

Black World Today

http://www.tbwt.com/

Be sure to load the images for this site so you don't miss anything. Here you'll find feature stories on vital issues in black America and in Africa; you'll also find news, views, and analysis; "Black Country Profiles"; black history; an "Inspiration Center"; global chat; and more. The Inspiration Center

intrigued me; I visited and found recommended links "that provide religious and spiritual material in a manner that we believe complements the information content." Those links include Christian, Buddhist, Jewish, and even Voodoo sites. The Black Country Profiles offer information about the politics, geography, climate, flora and fauna, population, cities, religion, education, economy, and other topics for several dozen African and Carribean nations. A most impressive site and a thorough site.

Of related interest: Black and Hispanic Resources

Business and Science News

http://www.businesswire.com

All the latest business news, organized by headline and with a search engine, in case you want to get new developments concerning a particular company or field. You'll find corporate news, as well as news from high-tech, medical, health care, pharmaceutical industries. You can also get a "media press kit" on any of hundreds of companies, universities, and organizations. This will provide you with massive background on any company in which you have an interest. An excellent resource. Fee services as well for corporate clients; these include access to newsletters and ways of delivering information about your company to other businesses.

CNN Interactive

http://www.cnn.com/

If you're like me and you believe there's no such thing as too much CNN, you'll love the CNN website, which delivers up-to-the-minute news from around the world. You get an easy-to-read menu of stories; topics include the United States, the world, showbiz, CNN, sports, politics, sci-tech, earth, health, and more. You can also download videos in Quicktime format. All you have to do is point, click, and pretend you're James Earl Jones saying, in those basso profundo tones, "This . . . is CNN."

RECOMMENDED

Electronic Newsstand

http://www.enews.com

Billed as the Web's premiere magazine site. Home to 200+ magazines, providing free content—sample articles, table of contents, some cover art. You can order subscriptions "at deep discount prices" or simply browse through the magazines they serve. I went to the online versions of the *Economist* (nine articles) and *Yoga Journal* (three selections, yoga archives, "About the Magazine," and more). A great way to learn new things, get story and market ideas, and discover new publications to read.

The site also includes a search engine covering 2,000 magazines, which you can search by name or subject, and links to all 2,000. I jumped to the *People Magazine* home page, but I could have gone just as easily to *Games First!* or *Vagabond Monthly.* Hmm. *Vagabond Monthly.* How do they keep track of their subscribers? Well, that's not our problem. Also a list of the "Enews top 20," the periodicals that attract the most attention. The top five are *Yellow Silk, Discover, Business Week, The New Republic,* and the *New Yorker.*

RECOMMENDED

Essays on Journalism

http://www.poynter.org

Fascinating, thoughtful, brilliant essays on journalism by writers like Jeff Klinkenberg ("Writing About Place: The Boundaries of a Story"), Christopher Scanlon ("The Clock Is Ticking: Techniques for Story Telling on Deadline"), and Donald M. Murray ("Real Writers Don't Burn Out: Making a Writing Apprenticeship Last a Lifetime"). This is joyous, first-class writing about journalism. It doesn't matter what your field is. If you want to increase your appreciation for good writing and be awakened by the sensitivities of excellent observers of human nature, speed your way to this site. From the Poynter Institute for Media Studies.

European Journalism

http://www.demon.co.uk/eurojournalism/

This is a fantastic site offering you links to breaking stories in Europe and tons of other Europe-related news resources. All you need to know, for example, about the war in the former Yugoslavia, the Northern Ireland peace process, the McLibel trial (McDonald's sued in English courts), and mad cow disease. You can also learn about the European Union, European broadcast media on the Net, newspapers, magazines, media gateways, and advertising agencies.

Fourth World Documentation Project

http://www.halcyon.com/FWDP/fwdp.html

A site for those interested in indigenous peoples whose nations have been subsumed into the larger political order. You'll find examples around the globe, on every continent. Wondering what to write about next? Why not drop in here and expand your worldview? Essays, policy statements, articles on traditional medicine, violence, Native Americans, and much more. I clicked on **Documents from Melanesia, Polynesia, and the Pacific** and found documents relating to Hawaii (spelled "Hawai'i" here), West Papua, and the Kanak Nation of New Caledonia.

Hispanic Magazine

http://www.hisp.com/

This online edition of *Hispanic Magazine*, a monthly national magazine with a circulation of 250,000, covers news, events, and issues of interest to the Latino community. The site offers top stories from the current issues, back issues, and a list of Latino-related websites called "Tesoros del Web." Also information on *Moderna*, a magazine for Latinas featuring articles on beauty, fashion, and health. The current issue at the time of my visit offered articles on whether Latino leaders "got the message" regarding a grassroots march on Washington, Latinos in cyberspace, and "magazine mania" in the Hispanic market. Well-written and informative. As the website says, saludos!

Of related interest: Black and Hispanic Resources

HotWired

http://www.hotwired.com

The absolute latest Net news ("How do you keep minors out of your smutty Web site and your butt out of jail?"), science stories, dream techie jobs, editorials, an archive of past stories, and free membership in HotWired Network—all the excitement and information of the leading, cutting-edge magazine about the Internet, on the Internet, right here. You can read stories here before they appear in the print version of *Wired* magazine.

Index on Censorship

http://www.oneworld.org/index_oc/

Although many of us enjoy a relatively free press, it's easy to forget that others don't. This excerpt from the Index on Censorship home page offers an overview of the Cuban press situation before and since the Castro revolution. This site has a link to the Index home page, but be warned: It's a slow ride, but a worthwhile one.

Latino Media

http://www.tristero.com/LatInfo/media.html

Links to several dozen media outlets covering the Latino world, in Spanish and English. You can find Mexican newspapers available via FTP, business information about Latin America, the *Texas Hispanic Business Journal,* "Local Times in the Americas," among other sites.

Of related interest: Black and Hispanic Resources

Los Angeles Times

http://www.latimes.com/

In addition to a host of newspaper features (news, weather, sports, backgrounders, restaurant reviews, and "Destination: L.A." for locals and visitors), you'll find a most useful research tool: a search engine that lets you search the entire archives of the *L.A. Times* back to 1990. You just enter a keyword or -words and the search engine presents you with the headline, the first few sentences of the story, the date, author, and length. You can print these citations for free, or you can order the entire article for $1.50. You can display them most recent first, oldest first, or most relevant (to the search criteria you present) first. Or you can use a research service at the *Times*; details available at the website. Because this is L.A., I searched for O.J. Simpson and found 403 articles. I tried a few other searches: Guatemala got 146 hits; airbags 3; rainbow, 173.

You can go directly to the search engine with this URL: *http://www.latimes.com/cgi-bin/archsearch-cgi*

MediaFinder

http://www.mediafinder.com/

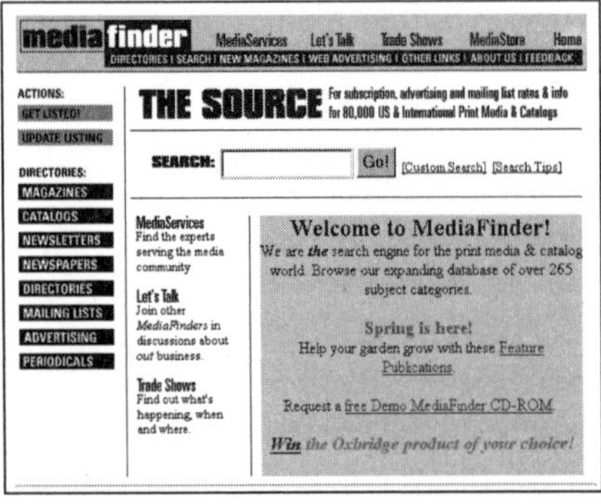

The main purpose of this site is to assist companies doing direct mail by locating magazines and other publications that rent lists of their readers. But if you write for magazines, you may find it helpful because you can search by topic for magazines and journals that may be too new to appear in the current *Writer's Market*. For instance, I searched two categories of new magazines: Under "Baseball," I found *Hardball Magazine*, which I'd never heard of; and "Health" turned up *Country Living, Healthy Living, Shape Cooks,* and *Wellness*—along with addresses, telephone numbers, and names of editors for all five. A useful adjunct to your current means of finding paying markets for your magazine pieces.

MSNBC—Microsoft-NBC News Service

http://www.msnbc.com/news/default.asp

Breaking and archived news about the world, commerce, sports, sci tech, life, and opinion. Interactive features include quizzes, maps, and timelines, allowing you essentially to participate more fully in your own education. I clicked in on a breaking story about an FBI agent arrested for and charged with selling secrets to the Russians (are there really any Russians left who can even afford secrets?) and got the story, a photo of the guy, a sketch from court, and an audio report from an NBC reporter. You can also personalize your MSNBC front page so that the news you want pops right up when you dial in.

The New York Times

http://www.nytimes.com/

The *Times* is currently available free online; they do ask you to register. All the usual features of the newspaper—news, sports, arts and leisure, book reviews, an archives section, and best of all, you can download software that lets you do *The New York Times* Crossword Puzzle on your own computer. You'll find forum sections that allow you to comment on the news—and send e-mail directly to other people in the thread. You'll also find CyberTimes, offering daily news updates on everything to do with computers and the Web. CyberTimes Extra includes information that does not appear in the printed version of the paper; it's for Web users only. At CyberTimes you'll also find *The New York Times* Navigator, "a guide to the Internet used by Times reporters and editors for research, exploration and fun." A new feature allows you access to thousands of current and past *New York Times* book reviews. Learn more in Chapter 14, "Review Sources."

News on the Web

http://www.cs.vu.nl/~gerben/news.html

An amazing reference: dozens of links to news sources around the world. You can read the *New York Times*, listen to National Public Radio, get White House briefings, page through the *Dallas Morning News*, read daily news briefings from the African National Congress in South Africa, catch up on the latest events in Eastern Europe . . . and never get newsprint on your fingers. Hundreds of fascinating links.

PBS NewsHour Online **RECOMMENDED**

http://www1.pbs.org/newshour/

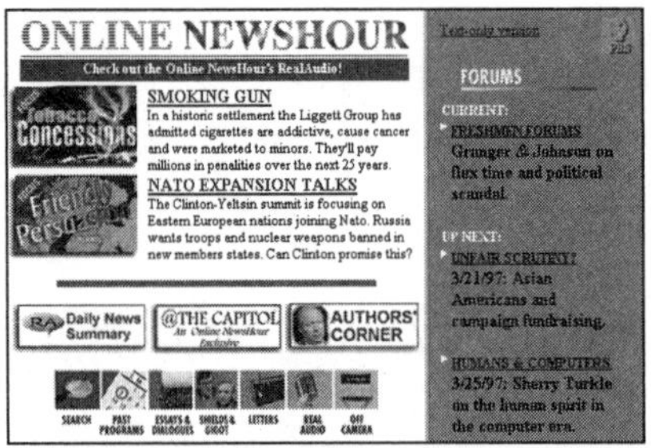

The daily news summary, feature stories, news forums, RealAudio segments of previous broadcasts, past programs organized by topic or region of the world (Africa, Asia, Law, White House, Religion, and so on), and a search engine bring the best of television news to your computer screen. I clicked on the **Race Relations** section of the "Past Programs" menu and found 23 transcripts of stories from the past year that ran on the NewsHour. Topics included discrimination at Texaco, California's anti-affirmative action Proposition 209, the Million Man March, interviews with newspapers, and more. RealAudio sound versions of the stories were also available. An excellent resource for journalists, nonfiction writers, or anyone who wants a highly regarded news source.

Poynter Institute for Media Studies Library Research Center **RECOMMENDED**

http://www.poynter.org/

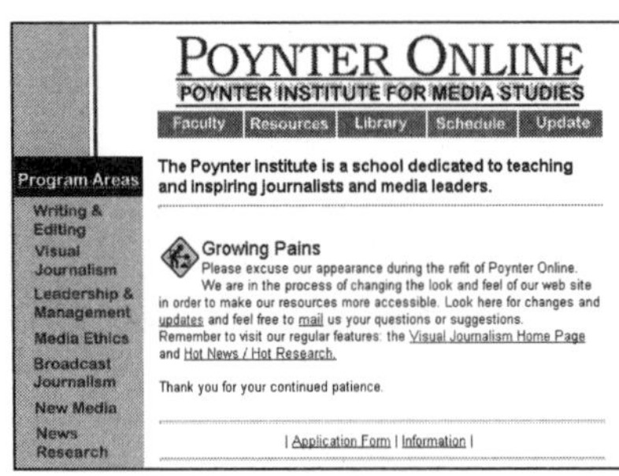

A marvelous reference site for journalists and anyone else interested in the world of news reporting, from the Poynter Institute for Media Studies. Click on **Files** and you'll come to a submenu offering articles, essays, and handbooks on topics like "Broadcast Journalism," "Campaign/Election Coverage," "Computer Assisted Reporting," "Ethics," and "Investigative Reporting." Go to **Bibliographies** and you'll find articles and books covering "Race and Gender," "Interviewing," "World Press," "New Media," "Media Leadership," and a dozen other topics. Click on **Hot News/Hot Research** and you'll find "research sources that will help you understand and cover top stories." When I visited, there were five excellent links recommended on each of these topics—the exodus in Zaire, the O.J. Simpson civil trial, and Yeltsin's health, along with dozens of other topics. For example, the five links offered for sites related to Yeltsin's heart condition were a chronology and biography of Yeltsin from a Russian news agency with headquarters in Moscow; updates and news concerning his recovery; a description of bypass surgery from the "Heart and Stroke Guide," described as "an excellent resource from the American Heart Association"; a profile of pioneering U.S. heart surgeon and advisor to Yeltsin's surgeons, Michael DeBakey; and a "Patient/Family Guide to Heart Surgery." Need I say more about the thoroughness and exciting quality of this site?

But I will, anyway: a stupendous resource, one of the most useful places on the entire Writer's Web. Rush there right away.

Statistics

http://www.nilesonline.com/stats

If you did about as well in math class as I did (I never finished high school trigonometry), if you shove your bank statements into a drawer with a promise that someday you'll go through them, if the idea of computing a 15% tip on a restaurant bill throws you into paroxysms of fear—this site is for you.

The brilliant Robert Niles has created a site defining all the math terms and topics that we writers ought to know about . . . but don't. These include standard deviation, margin of error, sample sizes, and more. I clicked on **Margin of Error** and was rewarded with a clear and readable essay on why polling data are often incorrectly reported and nonexistent trends become news stories. A great site.

Of related interest: Science, Technology, and Computer Writing

Wall Street Journal Interactive Edition

http://wsj.com

You can get the *Journal* online, but all features require a paid subscription. You can get a two-week, no-risk trial if you like. The *Wall Street Journal* is a phenomenal resource for writers, even for fiction writers who don't know their NASDAQ from their pork bellies. You'll find excellent writing on all topics related to modern life: business, certainly, but also trends, politics, arts, and the rest of the world. I'm never quite so happy as I am with a copy of the *Journal*; whether you get it online or in print, you'll have your ideas challenged and you'll get plenty of new ones. A vital resource for any writer.

Washington Post

http://www.washingtonpost.com/

Top news stories, screen shots of today's front page, easy access to every story in the paper edition, all editorials, and other features. These include a visitor's guide to Washington, a flat tax calculator, Federal Community, a "Home Base For Federal Workers," special reports on crime and drugs, a restaurant guide, a listing of top Washington-related websites, and a chatroom. Also offers links to business, international, and national news sources. Sports fans will find information about D.C.-area sports teams; college and pro sports news from the *Post* and the Associated Press; databases; and tons more. A great resource for anyone interested in government and politics.

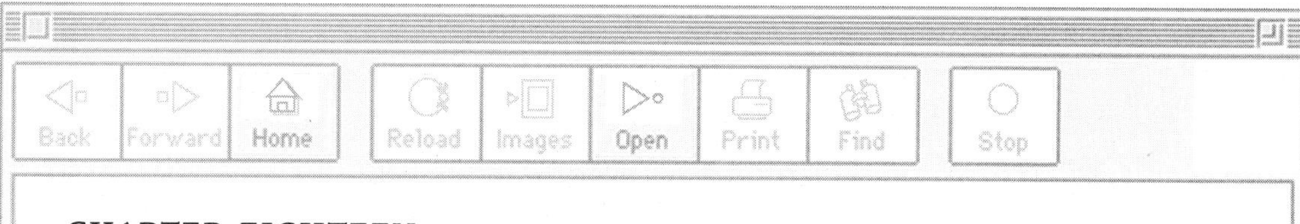

CHAPTER EIGHTEEN

MYSTERY WRITING

The two best pieces of advice I can give mystery writers: Put the dead body on the first page, or very close to it, and bookmark these excellent sites. Here you'll find the latest bestsellers, a search engine that lets you comb through mysteries searching by weapon, reviews, articles, and my favorite site in this section, "Mystery Writers' Reference Books," which offers up-to-the-minute ghoulish information that takes the, er, mystery, out of mystery writing.

Bibliomysteries

RECOMMENDED

http://www.carol.net/~lawrence/bibliomysteries/bibhome.htm

This site is entitled "Bibliomysteries"—those mysteries with "settings, plots, or substantial characters . . . related to the world of books, archives, and libraries." You'll find a wonderfully long list of such books with adorable icons indicating whether it's about, among other things, a bookstore or bookseller (a bag of money atop a green book), a writer (an old manual typewriter), a publisher (an old-fashioned printing press), or a library detective (a woman of a certain age, her hair in a bun).

You can also search by weapons that have been used in stories or "weapons that you would like to see," including an "OCLC terminal or other computer electrocution" or "poisoning by preservation chemicals." A joyous site for lovers of book-related mysteries.

Mystery Writers' Reference Books

RECOMMENDED

http://www.sodacreekpress.com/Mystery_Ref.html

This website reads, "Here is the book to make sure the gun in Chapter II is right for offing Aunt Felicity." Such is the description at this website for Michael Newton's *Armed and Dangerous: A Writer's Guide to Weapons*, one of several dozen reference books to add verisimilitude to any mystery writer's work. You'll also find *Body Trauma: A Writer's Guide to Wounds and Injuries, Scene of the Crime: A Writer's Guide to Crime Scene Investigation*, and *Deadly Doses: A Writer's Guide to Poisons.* How much fun is this? Also books by famous mystery writers, like Sue Grafton, on the art of writing mysteries. A killer website.

New Mysteries in Hardcover

http://www.freenet.vcu.edu/education/literature/newmyst.html

If you live from Sue Grafton to Sue Grafton or from Dick Francis to Dick Francis, now you can find out in advance when next your craving can be fulfilled. Drop into this thoughtful site and you'll learn who's coming out when, with what publisher, and for how much. It takes the mystery . . . out of buying mysteries.

Prairie Lights Review of Books

http://www.iowacity.com/icmag/BookReviews.html

A service of *Iowa City Magazine* providing reviews of half a dozen new mystery novels. I'm including it because I love the title. Prairie Lights. It's just so poetic. Call me crazy.

Of related interest: Review Sources

Skeleton Keys

http://www.slip.net/~cluelass/Opportunity.html

Articles and other references for mystery writers seeking to market their work. You'll find publishers seeking writers and an annotated listing, with e-mail or Web links, for venues that publish mystery writing. You'll find writing contests and awards with descriptions of who sponsors same; what the rules, prizes, and deadlines are; and e-mail or Web links to them. You'll find support groups for mystery writers, reference books, and a dictionary of "argot from the golden age of pulp." A lovingly designed site and a true service to mystery writers.

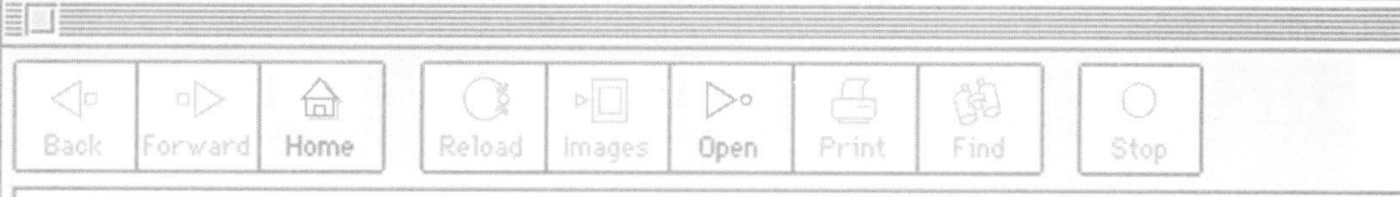

CHAPTER NINETEEN

POETRY

The Internet lends itself to the broad sharing of poetry because the traditional means—small, expensive private printings with limited distribution—isn't all that great. True, there's nothing like the feel of a book of poetry, especially if it's your own. But until you're ready to have your work bound for the ages, glory, and the bestseller list, you can find a massive audience, gain immediate feedback, meet other poets, and have fun.

It's my great pleasure to offer you a large number of sites where you can post your poetry, comment on the work of other poets, read about poetry, enter contests, and even find a rhyming dictionary. I'd like to add, based on recent conversations with editors at some of the nation's leading publishers, that one of the best-kept secrets of the publishing world today is that poetry is making publishers—and some poets—a lot of money. That's no reason to go into poetry, but poets should be compensated for their work just as much as any other author.

Aha!Poetry

http://www.faximum.com/aha!poetry

A clean, well-lighted place for poets. Here you can post your poems for "Open Mike Night," post an entire book of poems for others to read, read the books of others, get publishing information on small-press editions of poetry, learn about different forms of poetry (such as cinquain, ghazal, and tanka), find contests, take a poetry lesson . . . do you get the idea? If it scans, or rhymes, or is unmetered, or does whatever ghazal and tanka do, it happens here. Workshops and moderated poetry chats to follow soon. Ghazal, of course, is ancient Persian poetry, usually about erotic subjects. And tanka . . . well, if you want to find out how it's similar to a choka, you'll just have to see the site for yourself.

The AlienFlower Poetry Workshop

http://www.sonic.net/Web/albany/workshop/

Formerly the Albany Poetry Workshop, this site offers poets a place to hone their craft and share their work with others. You'll find poems, of course, and writing workshops, discussion groups, online classes, guidelines for critiquing poems, and some intriguing exercises that will help you grow as a poet. I like this site because it takes good poetry seriously. Worth your time.

American Academy of Poetry

http://www.he.net/~susannah/academy.htm

Founded in 1934, America's oldest resource supporting poets and poetry offers poems, information about National Poetry Month, membership information, press releases, and news of poetry awards that range from $100 to $100,000. This website is concise and thorough but provides only a limited amount of information about the Academy.

Codyco Poetry Contest

http://members.tripod.com/~codyco/index.html

This Nova Scotia–based group invites you to enter a poetry contest in any of three categories: politics, sports, and pets. You can enter two poems for $5 (Canadian, presumably) or five poems for $10; top prize is $100. I don't know who these people are, and they may be as straight up as my last martini, but remember that any time you send anyone money for something you see on the Internet, you're running a risk.

Internet Poetry Archive

http://sunsite.unc.edu/ipa/

A new way to appreciate and teach poetry: the Internet Poetry Archive, a gift to the Internet from various departments of the University of North Carolina, features selected poems, audio clips of poets reading their work, commentary, photos of the poets, and more. The initial poets represented are Philip Levine and Nobel Prize winners Seamus Heaney and Czeslaw Milosz. An attractive and thoughtful site; excellent for educators.

Irish Poetry Page

http://www.spinfo.uni-koeln.de/~dm/eire.html

The URL is actually a Gaelic expression that means, "Can you think of a two-syllable word that rhymes with Guinness?" Just kidding. Here you'll find the work of Irish poets including J.M. Synge, Oscar Wilde, William Butler Yeats, Seamus Heaney, and several dozen others. You'll also find Irish poems set to music; links to other Irish poetry websites; Library of Congress

bibliographies of the poets; and more. Sponsored, as you might have guessed, by the Department of Linguistic Data Processing at the University of Cologne, Germany.

Live Poets Society

http://www.catalog.com/cgibin/var/bartmon/welcome.htm

What a great name, for starters. And much more. Over 1,100 poets list their work; you can view theirs and comment on it or post your own. You can also read others' comments, venture into opinion forums, and find other poetry links. The site is updated every few days, and you can simply click on the date or dates you haven't read yet. You can also e-mail the authors directly with your thoughts. Poets who haven't contacted the site within six months are moved into an "expired" section. Clever, attractive, well designed.

Rhyming Dictionary

http://www.cs.cmu.edu/~dougb/rhyme.html

Courtesy of Doug Beeferman (rhymes with Slug Thief German), you can type in a word, any word, and ask the search engine to find "perfect rhymes," match last sound only, or find homophones. A wonderful tool for poets and lyricists. I don't think Slug Thief German is the sort of phrase that songwriters are straining to invent, but if you keep your requests under three syllables you'll be excited by what you find.

Spout Poetry Magazine

http://www.cs.man.ac.uk/peve/Staff/Jon/Poetry/spout.html

Spout comes to us from across the sea; you can join these English poets at their online workshop or you can simply read their work. The most recent issue of *Spout* is published online. You can publish your poetry in *Spout* if you join the workshop. I'm not sure that the work you'll find here is world-class, but it's certainly an opportunity to expand your readership. An earnest site.

t@p Poetry Slam

http://www.taponline.com/fringe/poetry/index.html

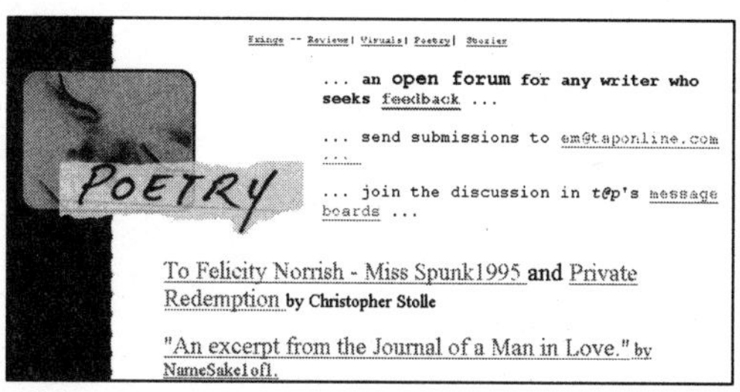

This large, commercial site is aimed at people in their 20s; the "fringe" area is for people that age who wish to post poetry and receive comments, read poetry and make comments, or laugh at poetry and make snide comments. But how cutting edge can a poetry site be if it's sponsored by Twizzlers? An actual excerpt: "My problem:/I just don't believe./Call it masturbation./Blame it on reality." I know—they're doing their best. I'd hate to look at the poetry I wrote when I was in my 20s.

Zuzu's Petals Quarterly Online—Poetry

http://www.lehigh.net.zuzu/zu-link.htm

A quarterly publication and an award-winning website publishing high-quality poetry, fiction, commentary, and book reviews. Also sponsors a semi-annual poetry contest, the proceeds of which "keep the magazine ad-free and available free of charge on the Internet." You can read entire issues of the magazine, a recent example of which contained solely poetry written by authors around the United States. Other issues offered short stories and essays. A classy publication. You can also find lots of fun here: word fun, games, anagrams, tests, trivia, "eyecandy," jokes, general humor, "serious diversions," and "food diversions" like "Pickles as a source of light." The site has an alphabetical list of all contributing poets.

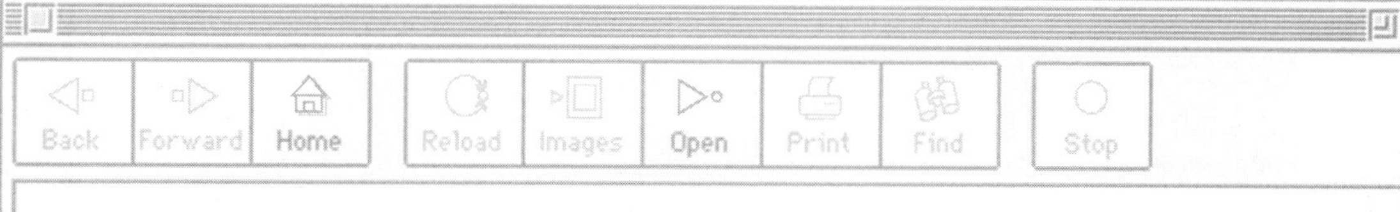

CHAPTER TWENTY

ROMANCE WRITING

Love is in the cyber-air at these sites. You can learn how to get started, how to get published, and how to get connected with other romance writers and readers. Romance writing is a fairly tightly knit community, which makes sense when you consider that this genre, perhaps above all others, is really all about one's feelings and about making connections with other people. If you are new to the genre, be sure to visit Linda Barlow's excellent website, Getting Started. Welcome to the heartland of the Internet.

A Garden of Delights

http://www.tlt.com/

The *Literary Times* of London recognizes the importance of romance novels in the lives of its readers. Here you'll find a chatroom, notices, news, and information about the romance genre; a research and reference center; information for romance authors seeking reviews; details on author itineraries; personal pages for romance authors; and more. You'll also find a feature called "Enchante"—"Romantic ideas and gift suggestions 'for the men in our lives, for the women in theirs.'" And a "Backlist Bookshelf" that lets you locate your favorite romance writers' previous books and order them instantly from amazon.com; and more services for the romance reader and writer. Somehow you don't associate the publication "Literary Times of London" with romance novels, but life is full of little surprises.

Getting Started

http://www.monash.com/writers.html

Linda Barlow, bestselling novelist and president of the Romance Writers of America, gives you precise and concise information about how to get started writing and publishing. If you want the truth, the whole truth, and nothing but the truth about agents, money, first-time writers, and other topics related to how you can make your way in the publishing world, start here. Ms. Barlow also offers thoughtfully chosen links to other excellent websites.

Harlequin Books

http://www.romance.net

I can explain romance novels to you, in case you're not an aficionado. They're all about getting a grip on men who have one-syllable first names like "Girk" and "Blang" and "Klog" and making them shave. If you have any more questions about romance novels, or if you'd like links to the home pages of dozens of their authors, or if you want your horoscope read, drop in. You'll also find excerpts from "I Can Fix It Myself" by Susie Tompkins in the "Susie's Helpful Hints" archive.

Write Page

http://www.writepage.com/

For readers and writers of genre fiction—sci fi, romance, historical, mystery, techno-thriller, and "weird." I dropped in on the Romance site because it gets lonely sitting at the office and staring into the Internet. There I found articles, links to a Reader's Guide to Romance & Women's Fiction, and an online issue of "Rawhide and Lace" for fans of Western romances. Also a long, long list of links to romance authors' websites. And a calendar for sale called "Studmuffins of Science" featuring "Ph.D.s with physiques to die for."

The best thing about this site is probably the links to the authors; by trying to cover every single genre, they may have given themselves too large a task. The history and romance lists of links are ample; murder mystery decent, sci fi fairly brief. A good starting point, nonetheless.

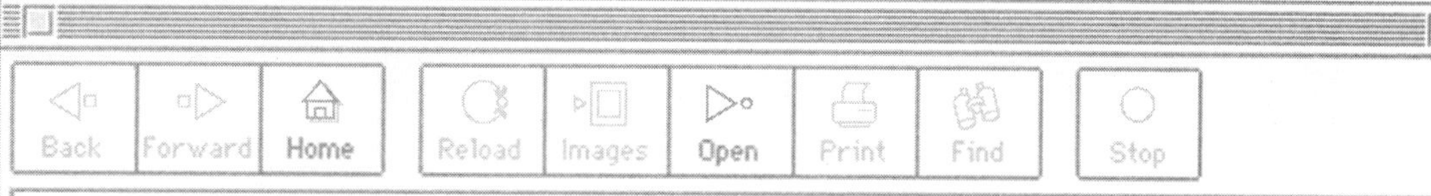

CHAPTER TWENTY-ONE

SCIENCE FICTION/ FANTASY/HORROR

Science fiction, fantasy, and horror writers are out there pushing their respective envelopes, making the world a little less comfortable and safe for the rest of us. And that's how it should be. Here you'll find—mostly against black backgrounds—websites offering reading lists, marketing information, writers' groups, Internet resources, and more links for those who don't scare easily.

Critters Workshop

RECOMMENDED

http://www.cs.du.edu:80/users/critters

An online "workshop/critique group" for serious science fiction/fantasy/horror writers. You send a story, chapter, or chapters of a novel through the workshop, and it goes out to at least 75 readers, many of whom are scientists and offer comments on technical accuracy. The website suggests that at least 15 readers offer comments and that their comments are much more specific and useful than "I liked it" or "I hated it." Critiques are expected within one week of the circulation of the material. If you have an entire novel you wish to circulate, you may ask for "dedicated readers" who wish to read it in its entirety. I'm impressed with the seriousness of purpose in this website and I thought the "sample comments" published on one of the inside Web pages was quite good. If you write science fiction or fantasy, perhaps you ought to be a Critter, too. Would Jimmy Durante say "Everybody's a Critter"? Hard to say.

DarkEcho's Horror Web

http://www.darkecho.com/

The home page begins, "A place spun in cyberspace for those who seek the darker side of fiction," and I'm too scared to disagree. Here you'll read the *DarkEcho Newsletter*, a weekly e-mail newsletter for horror writers and others; interviews with authors; an exploration into "The Perception and Psychology of the Horror Writer"; a horror writers' online workshop in which you can present your stories, read those of other horror writers, and offer comments; and "dark links" to other benighted corners of cyberspace. Presented with a wonderful sense of fun—red links against a black background, delightfully spooky.

Horror: 100 Best Books

http://www.cat.pdx.edu/~caseyh/horror/top100.html

Horror authors offer their top 100, in chronological order, starting with Christopher Marlowe's *The Tragical History of Dr. Faustus* and proceeding through Shakespeare, Jane Austen, Edgar Allan Poe, Bram Stoker, and many authors most general readers haven't before encountered. The latest authors to win acclaim are Ramsey Campbell, Robert McCammon, Charles N. Grant, and Lisa Turtle. This site offers links to a few pages focused on particular authors. A fine way for writers in any field to broaden their horizons.

Internet Top 100 Science Fiction/Fantasy Lists

http://www.clark.net/pub/iz/Books/Top100/top100.html

At the time of my first visit, Tolkien's *Lord of the Rings* won, *Ender's Game* by Orson Scott Card placed, and Frank Herbert's *Dune* showed in this survey of 1,456 voters. An excellent reading list for anyone new to the genres of science fiction and fantasy. Voters are sci fi readers who frequent the sci fi newsgroups. You can get copies of the lists, which are updated weekly—and you can vote for your favorites, too. With links to other lists of highly regarded sci fi and fantasy.

The Market List

http://www.members.aol.com/marketlist/index.html

Here you'll find over 100 markets for your science fiction, fantasy, and horror short fiction, categorized by pro, semi-pro, small press, e-zine, anthology, and contest. Each entry includes story length, pay rate, average response time, and general submission information. An attractive innovation allows you to search for markets that accept simultaneous submissions; you can also search by genre or by story lengths accepted. That's a brilliant idea and one that other lists of fiction markets should copy. I dipped into the semi-pro markets and found smaller publications like *Aberrations, Amelia, Blood & Midnight,* and *Freezer Burn Magazine* . . . which comes to you, not surprisingly, from Salem, Massachusetts.

Pittsburgh Worldwrights

http://www.cs.cmu.edu/~mslee/pw.html

A science fiction, fantasy, and horror writer's workshop currently with ten members, some of whom, according to the website, have published in leading magazines. You can read their work, visit their websites, or get to know them here. Find links to and information about paying science fiction/fantasy markets; a useful Q&A about how to sell in these genres; and information on rights, copyrights, small presses, and the utility of joining workshops like this one. A well-crafted, thoughtful, and entirely useful page, and a model for what other writing workshops can do for the entire community of writers on the Net.

Resources for Horror Writers

http://www.inkspot.com/genres/horror.html

This site is only accessible between midnight and daybreak. Just kidding. This is the true home of werewolves, vampires, and all things scary on the Net. You'll find links to several dozen websites that specialize in horror literature, three lists of horror writers with e-mail links to same, a mailing list for the creation and enjoyment of horror fiction, a list of the 100 best horror books, and even a section on vampires. Interestingly, both of the vampire lists use the spelling *vampyre.* (I've never seen that before, but the only horror I really know about is my social life.) A great place to start if you like scary things.

Science Fiction Links

http://nic2.hawaii.edu/~delbeek/scifi.html

This website takes you to dozens of science fiction resources and other collections of sci fi–related websites around the Internet. Point and click to be transported to well-chosen "Starting Points," information about television shows and movies, and sci fi art sites.

Usenet Newsgroups for Horror Writers and Fans

http://www.cat.pdx.edu/~caseyh/horror/thenews.html

Horror writers with time on their hands can explore the various newsgroups listed here. Remember that if these discussions don't satisfy, you can start your own newsgroup or you can visit *http://www.dejanews.com*, a super search engine for Usenet newsgroups: Type in a keyword to describe your interest, and find hyperlinks to newsgroups that contain your keyword. Some samples:

alt.books.annrice	Reviews of her books and movies
alt.vampyres	Vampire personals, quotes, jokes, and vampire stories
alt.horror	Warnings about disreputable literary agencies, movie reviews, and advertisements
alt.folklore.ghoststories	Many questions about the existence of ghosts and angels, stories about same, and some ads
rec.arts.sf.written	Queries and answers about the process of writing science fiction
rec.arts.sf.marketplace	Selling science fiction
rec.arts.sf.tv	Science fiction on the small screen
rec.arts.sf.fandom	Science fiction readers speak out
rec.arts.sf.movies	Science fiction on the big screen

CHAPTER TWENTY-TWO

SCIENCE, TECHNOLOGY, AND COMPUTER WRITING

Scientific Americans, Scientific Canadians, Scientific Japanese, Scientific Poles, and Scientific Swedes—not to mention everyone else on the planet with a technological bent—will enjoy these selected sites. Those who wonder what computer people are actually talking about when they start flinging all those technical terms will find answers in The New Hacker's Dictionary and the Online Dictionary of Computing. Happy (particle) trails!

Computer Industry News

RECOMMENDED

http://www.sjmercury.com/

The Wall Street Journal published a description of this site as "one of the best-organized and most accessible newspapers online, with special attention to Silicon Valley and computer-industry news." The *San Jose Mercury News* is the Silicon Valley newspaper, and you'll find all the late breaking news about the computer industry at this site.

Computer and Internet Online Books Index

http://home.earthlink.net/~jlutgen/cirob.html

If you've got a question about anything to do with computers and the Internet, do not pass go, do not collect two hundred dollars. Instead race directly to this marvelous site, which offers an alphabetical index of dozens of books published online (which means you can read them right now and for free) concerned with computers and the Internet. Titles include (these are the F's): *File Formats on the Internet: A Guide for PC Users*; *From Webspace to Cyberspace*; *FrontPage Unleashed*; and *The Future of Statistical Software*, which my girlfriend and I read to each other late at night. You'll also find "Electronic Documents online," which offers you reference titles in the realms of computers, science, and language. These include the Internet Encyclopedia, Hacker's Jargon, and the Encyclopedia of MUDs project. A vital resource for propellerheads.

The Craft of Scientific Writing

RECOMMENDED

http://darkstar.engr.wisc.edu/alley/

Engineers and scientists can visit this site and take a self-study course to improve their writing skills. It's all free and it's excellent. Also here: information on short courses (three to five days) on writing skills, preparing documents, and "smoothing the language." What's the point of discovering or inventing something if no one knows what the heck you're talking about? A superlative site.

Internet Resources for Technical Communicators

http://www.interlog.com/~ksoltys/techcomm.html

Here the technical writer will find books and reference sources; information on copyrights, desktop publishing, HTML, and language; mailing lists; newsgroups; online help and documentation; and other sorts of information of particular use. Dozens of recommended books concerned with all aspects of technical writing. An excellent list (with links) of discussion groups on copy editing, desktop publishing, Adobe Acrobat software, SGML, Microsoft Word products, and lots of other technical stuff.

The New Hacker's Dictionary

http://fount.journalism.wisc.edu/jargon/jargon.html

An online version of the highly regarded book that explains what hackers mean when they're online. You'll learn how hacker jargon works, how it's constructed, what hacker writing style consists of, the use of words like *mumble*, *sigh*, and *groan*, and tons more. A well-written, articulate work that shows the effects of hackerspeak on the English language. The website opens up with a plea for you to buy the actual book; but you'll certainly have a good time with this study of hackification; you'll have a very low quotient of disgustitude. Great fun.

RECOMMENDED

Online Dictionary of Computing

http://wombat.doc.ic.ac.uk

Got a computer term you just can't figure out? Want to win bar bets or impress the opposite sex with your ability to distinguish between ROM and RAM? You can look it up at this excellent online dictionary of computer terms. I looked up *Spam* and found that it's from the Monty Python "Spam" song and means "to post irrelevant or inappropriate messages to one or more Usenet newsgroups or mailing lists in deliberate or accidental violation of Netiquette." What's also great about this dictionary is that the computer terms it uses in its definitions are hyperlinked to their own definitions.

A quote from the spam definition shows just how knowledgeable, witty, and well written the authors of this dictionary are:

> It is possible to spam a newsgroup with one well- (or ill-) planned message, e.g. asking "What do you think of abortion?" on soc.women. This can be done by cross-posting, e.g. any message which is cross-posted to alt.rush-limbaugh and alt.politics.homosexuality will almost inevitably spam both groups. Posting a message to a significant proportion of all newsgroups is a sure way to spam Usenet and become an object of almost universal hatred.

Science Links via Galaxy

RECOMMENDED

http://doradus.einet.net/galaxy/Science.html

Science information from all corners of cyberspace, available here and organized with breathtaking clarity into these major topics: "Astronomy," "Biology," "Chemistry," "Geosciences," "Mathematics," and "Physics." Each of those topics breaks down into eight subcategories. Biology, for instance, offers you botany, cell biology, entomology, medicine, microbiology, paleontology, and zoology. Click on any of those subjects and you'll find related websites organized by these groupings: "Academic Organizations," "Collections," "Directories," "Events," "Non-Profit Organizations," "Organizations," "Periodicals," "Sights and Sounds." Thank you, Wayne Allen and Bruce Speyer, creators of Galaxy, for one of the best reasons to go online. Also offers a search engine and a means by which you can link your science-related site.

Scientific American

http://www.sciam.com/

Here you will find the text of the entire current issue of *Scientific American*. The "Explorations" archive section is a highlight of the page, offering articles on a wide variety of topics including the Internet, astronomy, tornadoes, the quantum world, and medicine. Also interviews, "Ask the Experts," bookmarks for science-related websites, and a marketplace section. Links within articles take you to related information.

RECOMMENDED

Technical Writing Page

http://techwriting.miningco.com

Thank you, Gary Conroy, for this outstanding introduction to technical writing, replete with countless links to technical and scientific websites of service to the technical writer. The resource list breaks down into these categories: magazines, organizations, desktop publishing, language, education, authors, multimedia, help systems, corporate, and miscellaneous. You'll find newsgroups, advice, tutorials, lists of further links, documentation standards, fonts for desktop publishing, and toolbook sites.

CHAPTER TWENTY-THREE

SCREENWRITING AND FILM

Here you'll find expert advice about breaking into screenwriting; interviews with top film industry people; databases, like Mr. Hollywood and the Internet Movie Database, that provide every conceivable bit of information about motion pictures; actual scripts of dozens of your favorite movies that you can read or print out; and screenwriters' groups, online and off, for you to join. I'm ready for my close-up, Mr. Gates.

Drew's Script-O-Rama

http://home.cdsnet.net/~nikko11/nontable.htm

Dozens of scripts yours for free right here. You can also find the first four drafts of the script for *Star Wars*. A lot of overlap with the screenplays available at Screenwriter's Heaven. Still, there might be something here that you can't get elsewhere.

E-Script

http://ourworld.compuserve.com/homepages/single_lane/escript.htm

Get professional advice on your screenplay by joining one of E-Script's international screenwriting seminars. You'll get one-on-one training from top screenwriters, and you'll also receive comments from other screenwriting students around the globe. These sessions cost money; the free information available at the site includes "Postings," a selection of seminar leaders' weekly comments on screenwriting, and the "E-Script Virtual Q&A," interviews with leading screenwriters.

Film Festivals

http://filmfestivals.com/

Whenever I think of film festivals, I think of people racing around chaotically in limos, people barking into carphones, crowded restaurants, long lines, and impossibly beautiful and unattainable starlets on the arms of well-tanned, cigar-chomping producers. If this appeals to you, why not visit this website and find out where all the film festivals around the globe take place, and when, and how you can be a part of them. Some festivals linked to this page: Cannes, London, San Sebastian, Tokyo, Utrecht, and Istanbul.

The Film Zone

http://www.filmzone.com/mainindex.html

A quirky website with features like "Ask Satan" questions about the movie industry; "Predict-O-Scripts," allowing you to write summer blockbusters; some scathing satire of the film industry; "Hot Air"—excerpts of reviews that read like parodies of reviews; a search engine; archives; and more. This site is great fun and worth a look.

Got Ya Covered

http://oldwww.qdeck.com/~gundersn/gotya/gotya.html

Some of the most impressive names in the screenwriting field—Lew Hunter (my writing teacher), Linda Seger, Syd Field, and others—will review your screenplay for a nominal fee. If you want feedback from the best, this is where to go. These folks have written the leading books on screenwriting; you can consider the fee the equivalent of tuition for a one-on-one writing class. You'll also find here the useful "Ten things I look for in a script as a freelance reader."

The Hollywood Writer

http://www.io.com/~dbrown/TheHollywoodWriter.html

Some fairly realistic, if discouraging, advice for anyone thinking of packing up and moving to L.A. to pursue the dream. "There isn't any easy money to be had," one comment begins. "You can't come out here expecting, well I have a film degree, I'm going to find a job tomorrow in the film industry and on the side I'm going to write. Well, you're probably not going to find a job in the film industry tomorrow, and you're probably not going to find a job in three months or six months unless you're prepared to do secretarial work, some kind of office clerical work. Those jobs are abundant." Or, "If you send out 100 letters, you may get one positive response." As they say in 12-step-land, "Thank you for sharing." Worth a look if you need some negativity to give you something to kick against.

Hollywood Writers Network

http://www.hollywoodnetwork.com/hn/writing/index.html

Part of the massive Hollywood Network website, this site offers expert advice from the pros, columns, newsletters, a directory of agents, books and software, and more. Some of the services require free membership; information is available at the site. I checked into the Writers' Lounges and found chatrooms on a wide variety of subjects, from Actors and African-American entertainers to TV Talk and Writers.

I also visited the informative "Do's and Don'ts for Writers—How to Write Query Letters and Log Lines," which features Q&A about screenplay writing and selling; you can read the previous Q&As or offer your own. The writing columns offer articles about top writers, directors, producers, and executives. You can also listen to interviews with other top pros. There's a gift shop, books you can order, and links to a broad range of entertainment-related information sites in the Hollywood Network.

The Inkwell

http://TheInkwell.com/

Why is *War and Peace* so hard to make into a movie? What stories lend themselves better to film? Intriguing answers to these and other thoughtful questions at this screenwriting site. Here you'll find the first installments of "From Idea to Screen: A Guide to Writing a Script"; the full text of Aristotle's *Poetics*, which many screenwriting teachers insist is the best introduction available to the art of storytelling; names and addresses (but not phone numbers or contact people) for a long list of major production companies; and a listing of agencies "which I know can advance a writer's career." This is worth a visit.

RECOMMENDED

Internet Movie Database

http://us.imdb.com/

Bills itself as "The most comprehensive free source of movie information on the Internet." Over 1,250,000 filmography entries in this database, with details on everything and everyone in the film universe. Search by actors, directors, writers, composers, cinematographers, editors, production designers, costume designers, producers, and even sound recording directors, make-up designers, and color consultants. You'll also find 85,000 titles in the Internet Movie Database with credits for each of those pictures. Click on *Citizen Kane*, for instance, and you'll find a plot summary, trivia, quotes, locations, literature, soundbites, and tons more. A search engine will find anything in the movies and bring it back home to you. I clicked on **Danny DeVito** and found a complete filmography, his biography, an interview, notable TV appearances, and the name of his agent. If you visit this site, bring the jumbo popcorn, because you'll be in here for a while.

Movie Scripts Home Page

http://www.alaska.net/~danielh/Scripts/

Scripts for your reading pleasure. A small assortment, most of which are available at Screenwriter's Heaven, reviewed nearby. You will find here the scripts for films by James Cameron, David Lynch, and Quentin Tarantino, among others. The good news is that the screenplays are identified by author; the bad news is that they aren't in alphabetical or any other kind of order.

Mr. Showbiz

RECOMMENDED

http://Web3.starwave.com/

The ultimate information-packed, up-to-the-minute Hollywood website. You'll find today's Hollywood news; interviews with top stars and directors with films in current release (at the time of my visit, Michelle Pfeiffer, Penny Marshall, Denzel Washington, and Whitney Houston); box office, TV ratings, and music sales; reviews of movies, music, TV, and newly released video; an "Ask Mr. Showbiz" feature that lets you ask questions and receive information about the film industry and its denizens. Also extremely useful for screenwriters or for anyone who loves movies: detailed biographies and filmographies of top actors, directors, writers, comedians, TV personalities, models, musicians . . . I'm out of breath. One great site.

RealAudio Screenwriting Tips

http://www.teleport.com/~cdeemer/tip-home.html

The joke in Hollywood is that nobody reads anything; so if you find reading even screenwriting tips too taxing, you've got a bright future in the movie industry. In the meantime, you can listen to Charles Deemer's 12 tips on the craft of screenwriting via RealAudio. These include "The Zen of Screenwriting"; "Ponder Before You Pay"; "Being Patient with Your Story"; and "The Chainsaw Is Your Friend."

Recommended Reading List for Screenwriters

http://www.ourworld.compuserve.com:80/homepages/lgrantt/Research.htm

The best books and periodicals for screenwriters, with a brief description of each. Missing: *Screenwriting 434* by Lew Hunter, my writing teacher. An excellent book on writing for the movies, or for any genre.

Screenplay Format

http://www.vcu.edu/artweb/playwriting/screenformat.html

What should a screenplay look like? Find out fast by visiting this website. You'll get specifics about margins, titles, and the whole shebang at this page. With reviews and suggestions regarding screenplay formatting software.

RECOMMENDED

The Screenscribe—Hollywood Links

http://www.geocities.com/Hollywood/4486/

What's shaking at the studios? Find out for yourself at this delightfully Hollywood list of links. You'll find links to the home pages of all the top studios, the networks, current TV shows and films, and movie-related sites like Roger Ebert's Movie Reviews, Microsoft's Cinemania, Movies.Com, and The Film Zone. Have your server call my server, and let's do lunch.

Of related interest: Lists of Links

Screenwriter's Discussion Group

listserv@tamvm1.tamu.edu

According to film-in-cyberspace expert Charles Deemer, you'll get about 100 messages or more a day, some of which can be very helpful to you. To join, e-mail the above address and write the following message: **subscribe scrnwrit *Yourfirstname Yourlastname***

Of related interest: Mailing Lists and Newsgroups

Screenwriters FAQ

RECOMMENDED

gopher://gopher.panam.edu/11gopher_root12%3a%5bfaq%5d

Jack Stanley at the University of Texas-Pan American in Edinburg, Texas, has pulled together a vast amount of information about screenwriting. Topics include art versus commercialism; agents; books; contests and fellowships; copyright/registration; legal matters; magazines; options; script sources; script format; seminars and workshops; computer services (described below); Writers Guild of America; and Writing Tips.

To give you a sense of what a chapter contains, I took a long look at Chapter 14, on software, e-mail, and BBSs. I found screenwriters' comments on specific script-writing programs, story construction software, e-mail lists, and bulletin board services for screenwriters. It's like sitting in on a knowledgeable discussion with the pros. You'll hear about real-life experiences with the various products and services from writers who are in the trenches and not just speculating. Provocative and interesting.

Screenwriter's Heaven

RECOMMENDED

http://www.impactpc.demon.co.uk/

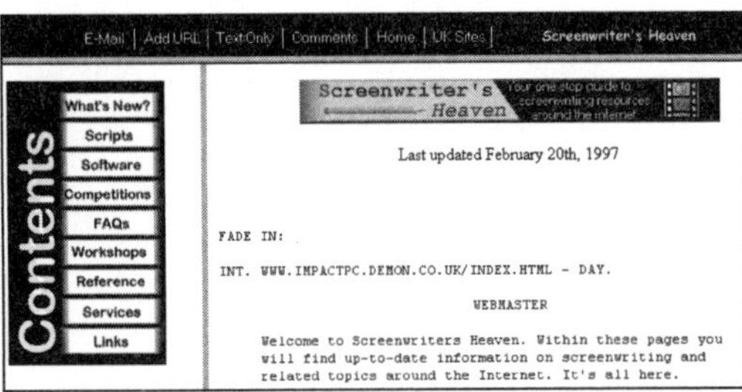

The title of this website reminds me of a cartoon: Inscribed on a screenwriter's tombstone were the words, "Would you read my screenplay?" If only that screenwriter could have visited Screenwriter's Heaven. There he or she would have found a massive listing of everything screenplay-related in cyberspace.

You'll find an A–Z listing of screenplays that you can read via the Internet—it even tells you if you're looking at a first draft, shooting script, director's revision, or transcript. Scripts available include classics like *Dr. Strangelove*, *The Godfather*, *Annie Hall*, *Star Wars*, and more recent films like *The Silence of the Lambs*, *The Lion King*, *Interview with the Vampire*, and *Natural Born Killers*. This is so amazing—you just click on the name of a film, and boom, there's the script. How can science fiction possibly compete with the reality of the Internet?

But this site offers even more. You'll find extensive links to screenwriting software websites, some of which offer free screenplay-formatting software (see ScriptRighter in this section); news of at least ten screenwriting competitions around the globe; FAQs about screenplays, screenplay formatting, principles of story construction, and more; and a breathtaking array of screenwriting links.

Be patient, because this site comes to you all the way from England and is jammed with excellent and well-chosen links. Truly deserves its title.

The Screenwriter's Master Chart

http://members.aol.com/maryjs/scrnrite/htm

What's supposed to happen, and when? Mary Shomon, screenwriter and humor writer, walks you through the various moments in the development of screenplays and tells you what they mean and when they're "supposed" to happen. These include the setup, the choice of path, the turning point, the moving forward metaphor, the post-point moment, and a lot of other terms that may or may not help your screenwriting but will certainly dazzle impressionable starlets you meet at Hollywood parties. Just remember not to say "I'm a screenwriter." Say, "I'm a producer."

RECOMMENDED

Screenwriters & Playwrights Home Page

http://www.teleport.com/~cdeemer/scrwriter.html

Billed as "The original resource for scriptwriters on the Internet (since 1994)"—and what a wonderful resource it is. You can find information on several dozen vital topics for screenwriters, including dramatic structure, screenplay format, writing the script, sample treatment, marketing, agents, contests, books, analyzing scripts, tips from pros, stagecraft, live chat, stage plays online, and much more. I clicked on **Tips from Pros** and found essays and interviews such as "Writing For Low Budget Films"; an interview with William Martell; "How NOT to Write a Screenplay"; interviews on becoming a director or producer; interview archives from various industry publications; and advice from a development producer.

You could get the equivalent of a master's degree in film from this one website. Includes RealAudio tips, a search engine, and beaucoup more. A joyous site for anyone who loves film.

Of related interest: Drama and Playwriting

ScriptRighter

http://www.fetching.com/scriptrighter/

Visit this site and you can download for free this version of ScriptRighter, the popular and highly successful screenplay-formatting software for Windows. The man behind the software, Lincoln Stewart, has since moved on to the independent cinema business and writes that he no longer has the time to update the software. Thus he makes it available to you, at no charge. There's no support available, but there is a user's bulletin board that allows you to swap suggestions with other ScriptRighter screenwriters.

Scripts & Screenplays

http://hollywoodu.com/script.htm

More scripts, available for free reading or printing—actually more overlap with Screenwriter's Heaven, but why not give you all the options?

Scripts On-Screen

http://www.scripts-onscreen.com/index.htm

This commercial site allows you to post screenplays and television scripts so that producers can take a look at them; the site claims that it has led to three screenplays being optioned and that 16 writers have found representation. It also sells screenplays and books on screenwriting and provides bios of the screenwriters whose work is available. If you go to *http://www.scripts-onscreen.com/treat.htm*, you'll find a brief, well-written, and useful guide to "Writing Better Log Lines and Treatments."

RECOMMENDED

ScriptTutor

http://scripttutor.com/

This excellent and fulsome site gives you tons of excellent information about screenwriting. Recognizing that form is the first thing a professional reader notices about a piece of writing, this site shows you how to make your work look thoroughly professional. One of the best features is the section "What not to do with your screenplay," offering tips like "Do not use a graphic on your cover page, or anywhere else in your screenplay"; "Do not use unusual fonts, bold or italic text, light printing, or anything else that makes your script difficult to read"; and "Do not number your scenes." Information also on graphics, fonts, character names, and other essentials. This is all part of the "Now Showing" section of the website.

As if that weren't enough to make this site special (it is), you'll find a great calendar of events of interest to screenwriters, a newsletter, script books, and script tips, including (here's the commercial part) a remarkably thorough script analysis service and a screenwriter's bookstore. An excellent site for anyone new to the business and craft of screenwriting.

Sundance Film Institute

http://www.cybermart.com/sundance

Sundance was founded in 1981 by Robert Redford to support independent filmmaking. The website offers information about the institute and its calendar, artistic programs, and news of the Sundance Film Festival, where new independent American films are given their premieres. Films like *sex, lies, and videotape, House Party, Gas Food Lodging, Like Water for Chocolate*, and *Hoop Dreams* were all discovered at the festival. If you're interested in entering a film at Sundance or if you want to attend the festival, you'll find all the information you need right here.

Tip Sheet For Low-Budget Film Scripts

RECOMMENDED

http://www.magic.ca/ffp/tips.html

This is a brilliant idea: Gather together in one place all the bugaboos that cause low-budget film scripts to be rejected for financial reasons. Written eloquently by Colin Brunton, producer, director, and currently executive producer for The Feature Film Project of the Canadian Film Centre. Brunton acknowledges that some of his suggestions are obvious, but even his explanations of the seemingly obvious teach a great deal about the realities of filmmaking. Topics include too many speaking parts, too many locations, SFX and firearms, exteriors on public roadways, night exteriors, crowd scenes, period pieces, trains and cars, animals and children, insurance, weather and seasons, and many more. This is well worth your time.

Ultimate Television

http://www.utv.net

Everything about TV but a remote and a couple of slices of pizza. You'll find today's news about TV and the entertainment community. Features at the time of my visit included reviews of shows; Golden Globe award previews, a Top Ten of the year's TV shows; articles about actors and writers; and columns on sports, soaps, kid vid, and cable. There is a calendar of videos to be released this week. You'll also find links to TV shows, as well as links to TV-related websites or basic information about TV for practically every country in the world. And a chat room. And a TV schedule, of course.

Of related interest: Print Periodicals

Voices of Experience

http://www.teleport.com/~cdeemer/Experience.html

Well-chosen essays, brought to you by webmaster Charles Deemer, discussing topics of importance to screenwriters. You'll find articles on agent scams, surviving as a freelancer, producers, the art of pitching, making the Hollywood film, the agent-writer relationship, and much more.

Of related interest: Essays on Writing and Publishing

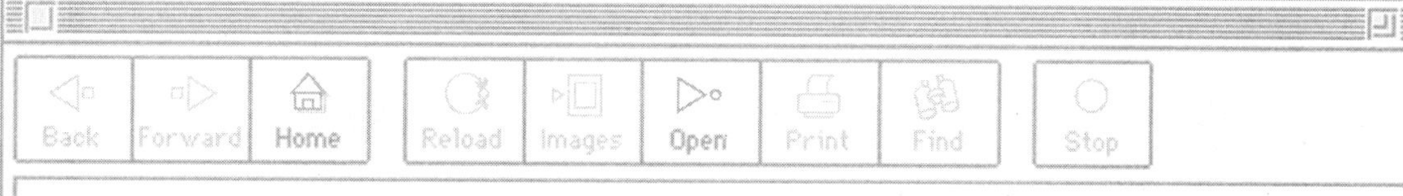

CHAPTER TWENTY-FOUR

CLASSES ONLINE

Listed below are writing classes that take place via the Internet. Universities and extension programs are just beginning to take advantage of cyberspace as a means of reaching new populations of students.

I taught online for the UCLA Writing Program for an entire year and found the experience really quite wonderful. Although the give-and-take of a classroom is lost, much is gained. First, students who can't drive to a campus every week can take part. These include parents of young children, people with heavy workloads, and people who live many miles from campus. Second, I found people getting a lot more intimate in their online writing than many students do in the classroom—probably because online classes offer a certain privacy that classrooms do not. So if you're wondering whether online classes can help you, the answer is, quite possibly, yes.

These folks are the pioneers. Others are likely to join soon.

Cyberspace Writing Center Consultation Project

http://fur.rscc.cc.tn.us/cyberproject.html

Two schools in Arkansas and Tennessee have a joint project through which composition, literature, and technical writing students at one school e-mail their class essays to grad students in rhetoric and writing at the other. The students then meet in a virtual reality setting where they can discuss the paper and "paste revisions directly into their conversation." The benefits flow both ways: The community college students get the wisdom of grad students and the grad students get teaching experience. Everybody wins. For more information on the program, or to find out how to set up a similar arrangement for schools in your area, drop by this site.

UCLA Writers Program Online

http://www.ucla.edu

The UCLA Writers Program offers ten-week classes in fiction writing and screenwriting taught by leading practitioners in those fields. The current courses include "Writing the Novel the Professional Way: A Works-in-Progress Online Workshop," with Dennis Foley; Creating Dynamic Scenes: An Online Workshop for Screenwriters, Playwrights, and Fiction Writers," with Paula Cizmar; and Introduction to Comedy Writing for Film and Television: Online," with Alicia Schudt. More classes are coming online each quarter. You can get a current schedule and registration information here. Disclaimer: I've taught in the UCLA Writers Program for the past seven years and think extremely highly of the Program and of my colleagues.

Virtual Crime Writing Workshop

http://theodore-sturgeon.MIT.EDU:8001/~cbrooks/crime3.html

Take this three-week "taster" (British English, presumably, for sample or trial) course with English author Clive Brooks. Course is a discussion seminar in a MOO with other students and includes a writing assignment in the Sherlock Holmes genre. A MOO, incidentally, is a real-time experience where you can move around, speak, and hang out with other library visitors. You reach it by Telnet. Take the class and move on to the twelve-week version, which "develops all the skills necessary for the creation of classic crime fiction short stories set in 1890s England." Offered through Diversity University, this site has maps, readings, period images, and e-mail lectures and assignments. Sounds like fun, doesn't it?

Of related interest: Mystery Writing

Writers on the Net

http://www.writers.com/

Online classes, tutors, and writing groups for poets, business writers, fiction writers, screenwriters . . . everybody. Several dozen classes when I visited, including Introduction to Poetry; How to Write and Sell a Contemporary Romance Novel; and Mystery, Thriller and Suspense Writing. You'll find dates, times, information about the classes, and background on the instructors.

Writing Tutorials: Distance Education for Talented Youth

http://jhunix.hcf.jhu.edu/~ewt2/

From Johns Hopkins University. Eighth through twelfth graders are invited to improve their writing skills with online courses that run from October through May. Each course contains 14 writing assignments; 800 students are enrolled this year, and nearly 6,000 have taken the course since 1983. Fiction and poetry. The course is described as "an intensive, rigorous academic experience" and works best with students who are "highly motivated, intellectually adventuresome, and ready to work." Every 10 to 14 days, a tutor mails the student a new assignment, a letter, and a commentary on the previous work. This sounds wonderful for students who want to write but haven't found the appropriate writing teacher in their own communities.

Of related interest: Young Adult, Middle Grade, and Children's Writing

CHAPTER TWENTY-FIVE

COPY EDITING SITES

Copy editing is an art form, and its practitioners are some of the greatest lovers of the English language. Every writer owes an enormous debt to the individuals who have cleaned up their occasional lapses in grammar and usage. Every unpublished writer makes the grave error of assuming that the quality of his or her ideas will overcome a limited or poor knowledge of the basics of English.

I frequently remind my students that every good literary agent or editor can do one of two things with a manuscript—either read it or proofread it. And once they start proofreading, they are on their way to rejecting the piece. The moral of the story: Writers who sincerely want to publish would do well to study the sites in this section. Good sentences make agents and editors happy. Happy agents and editors are the kind you want in your writing life.

Copy Editor

RECOMMENDED

http://www.copyeditor.com/Links.html

A site to gladden the bibliophile's eyes. The online version of the award-winning newsletter among whose 2,000 subscribers are the *New York Times* and Oxford University Press. Copy Editor focuses on the way the English language changes. Typical topics: new words, "sticky" style questions, interviews with leading copy editors, and updates on usage and style. At the Website you can download a sample issue, subscribe, and find workshops, links, and even jobs for copy editors.

The Copyediting-1 Style FAQ

http://www.rt66.com/~telp/sfindex.htm#q

Ever lain awake at night (or laid awake, or lay awake) staring at the ceiling, trying to decide whether an ending comma or period should be placed inside or outside quotation marks? Or whether A.D. precedes or follows the year? Or how to form a possessive for a word like "McDonald's"? You too? Well, we can recommend either the singles page in the *New York Review of Books* or this FAQ, which offers numbingly intricate answers to these nagging grammatical questions. You'll find not only the answers but the rules—and the paragraphs where they appear in the various style guides out there. Feel free to visit the site; but if you drop an apostrophe in a possessive in their presence, don't say I didn't warn you.

Magazine Copy Editing

http://www.well.com/user/mmcadams/copy.editing.html

The syllabus and reading list for a course on magazine copy editing, as prepared by Mindy McAdams, for New York University's Management Institute. The author has worked for *Time Magazine*, the *Washington Post*,

Dell, Doubleday, and Warner as a copy editor. She notes that she has "never taught this class online, and am not interested in doing so. If you would like to learn to edit, please read the books I have recommended; they will get you started." She also suggests that anyone interested in copy editing as a career can get an overview of the profession from the syllabus and the reading list.

Reference Books: A Bibliography for Copy Editors

http://www.well.com/user/mmcadams/reference.html

This site offers you annotated lists of reference books, style guides, dictionaries, almanacs, and other reference works for those who wield the editorial pencil. If you're not sure which reference book to buy or to rely upon, check out these authoritative listings.

RECOMMENDED

The Slot: A Spot for Copy Editors

http://www.theslot.com/

Bill Walsh, copy desk chief of the *Washington Times*, presents what started out as "The Crusty Old Man's Copy-Editing Peeve Page" and has since evolved into a wonderful guide for journalists and other writers to solving knotty problems in grammar, style, and sensitivity. Topics include word choice, capitalization, punctuation, reader-friendliness, quotations, matters of sensitivity, headlines, captions, and "Walshisms"—"those things that, while generally accepted as editing gospel, strike me as fishy." An entertaining and informative site for anyone who loves newspapers, English, or both.

A Spot for Copy Editors
By Bill Walsh

Of related interest: Journalism Resources

WebMaster

http://www.cio.com/central/style.html

Thirteen (at this writing) links to Web style guides covering everything from journalism to HTML. With well-written annotations that describe what you'll find at each site. The authors of the various guides are individuals, corporations, and think tanks. Visit them or offer your own. A service of *WebMaster* magazine.

WiredStyle

http://www.hotwired.com/hardwired/wiredstyle/toc/index.html

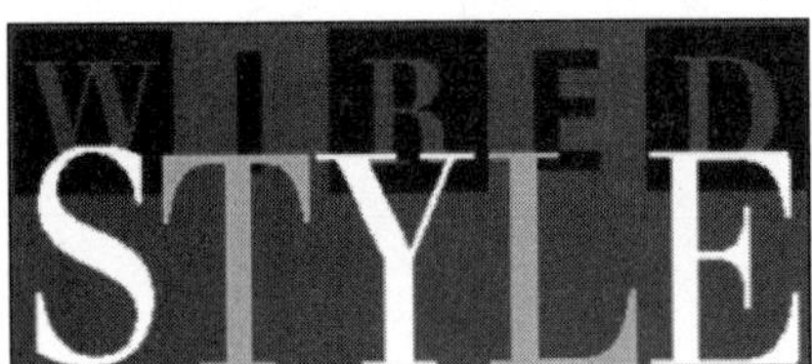

The new rules for the new world of writing. This website started as a discussion group among *Wired* editors to determine how best to handle the neologisms and other byproducts of the Internet age. Those discussions were formalized in a book, which you can order here. And then the book evolved into a website, where you can join the discussion on what words mean on the Internet. The entries are hip, thought-provoking, and entertaining. A painless way to improve your style.

Back Forward Home Reload Images Open Print Find Stop

CHAPTER TWENTY-SIX

GRAMMAR AND USAGE GUIDES

What's the difference between copy-editing sites and grammar/usage guides? If your work is accepted for publication, a copy editor will most likely have at it with a green pencil to check correctness, concision, and clarity—that's their job. Grammar and usage are *your* job. Dozens of grammar guides exist in cyberspace; I viewed them all and brought you the best. You'll find wonderful guides to writing, and you'll also find a couple of classics in the field. And, if you write scholarly works or papers for school and you need to know how to create citations to what you find in cyberspace, you'll learn how here.

Basic Prose Style

http://www.rpi.edu/dept/llc/writecenter/web/text/proseman.html

Prose style, punctuation, and mechanics take center stage at this website from the Rensselaer Polytechnic Institute. Craig Waddell walks you through suggestions like "Write in the Active Voice"; "Avoid Nominalizations"; "Express Parallel Ideas in Parallel Grammatical Form"; and "Always Wear Long Underwear When the Wind-Chill Hits Thirty Below." Okay, so I made up the last one. So flame me.

Citation Formats

http://www.cc.emory.edu/WHSCL/citation.formats.html

Let's say you're working on a paper for school, a research project, or a scholarly article, and you find just the source you need somewhere in cyberspace. How do you give credit where credit is due? You can find the answer quickly by visiting this website. Here you'll find several dozen links to sites explaining how to cite in bibliographies or notes work you've discovered on the Internet. My favorite is that of Janice Walker: MLA-Style Citations of Electronic Sources. It is reviewed below.

The Elements of Style

http://www.columbia.edu/acis/bartleby/strunk/index.html

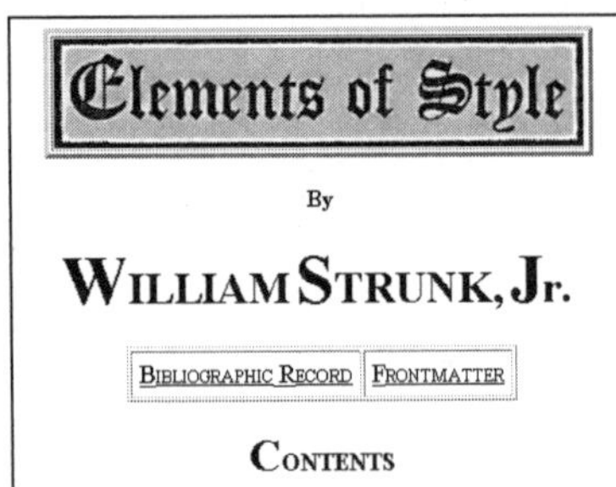

This is apparently the entire text of the first edition (1918) of the classic guide to standard written English, which in its current incarnation as "Strunk and White" is recommended to writing students everywhere—especially in my classrooms at UCLA and NYU. Clear, concise suggestions about how to write. If you're planning on being an arrogant, nasty fiction writer, first take these rules to heart lest you be accused of being all hat and no cattle.

I assume that Columbia is posting the first edition and not the current one for copyright reasons. (Why do I assume this? Check the sites listed in Chapter 9, "Copyright.") This website will give you a taste for the current edition, if you haven't yet read it.

Focusing On Words

http://www.wordfocus.com/#Focusing on Words

A delightful site for language lovers where you can "Experience the wonder of words and the English language." You'll find vocabulary programs that expand—and test—your knowledge of the subtleties of English vocabulary words. When I dropped in, I found a 20-question test on "Sensory Words"—words that express "feeling, sensation, perception through the senses, being aware, discerning." You then press a button to calculate your score, and a moment later, your score comes back and you can find out how smart you really are. Every time I've revisited the site, I've found more and more features, tests, essays, articles, and options. Currently there are some 20 word activities; I'm sure there will be more by the time of your visit. Don't expect to leave quickly. You'll want to stay and play and play and play.

Grammar Clinic Online

http://www.lydbury.co.uk/grammar/

Here you can post and riposte with other grammar-minded Netsurfers. You can offer your questions about proper usage of words and phrases or answer the questions that others have posted. "Toward" versus "towards," present participles, "over the last century" versus "in the last century."

Grammar and Style Notes

http://www.english.upenn.edu/~jlynch/grammar.html

Semicolons trouble? Been caught dangling your participle? Why not visit this writing site that offers brief, well-written, and accurate essays on grammar and usage topics like "Adjectives and Adverbs"; "And/or"; the Dash; Dependent versus Independent clauses; and many more topics. Questions answered here: Why do long words often indicate bad writing? What's the right way to use parentheses? This is a super site. The only problem with grammar books and style guides is that you're preaching to the choir—only people who already know (and care) about these things will drop by. Nevertheless, this is a wonderful site and criticism of it is something up with which I will not put.

The King's English by H.W. Fowler (1918)

http://www.columbia.edu/acis/bartleby/fowler

A million years ago (which is to say in the early 1970s), Manhattan offered the wandering booklover countless antiquarian bookstores run by people who looked about as old, dusty, and well read as the books they sold. Whatever happened to those people and those places? I think Starbucks bought up all the real estate, and the proprietors all moved on to that great reading room in the sky. I mention all this because on one such peregrination through the East Twenties during the second (and all-too-brief) Nixon administration, I found a beautiful blue copy of this very book. It answered most of the questions a young writer might ponder, such as when to use comparatives and superlatives, that and who and which, shall and will, and conditionals. It did not answer some of the other questions I had, which all came down to "How do I get Karen Pakula to notice me?" Well, you can't get everything out of one book.

The Bartleby Project at Columbia has posted a copy of this wonderful book, and now anyone with Internet access can learn about the gerund, debatable questions, the "spot plague," and substantial clauses. A delightful guide to good grammar.

Literature Webliography

http://www.lib.lsu.edu/hum/lit.html

General guides to literature, bibliographies, catalogs from around the world, dictionaries (including a "reverse dictionary," where you type in the definition and the dictionary gives you the word), periodicals, style guides, and texts from Louisiana State University. A list of links are here, many of which we've visited and described for you. This site is worth a visit if you want a good list of scholarly publications, information about Louisiana authors, an index of 20,000 periodicals, and access to library systems around the United States.

The Logical World of Etymology

http://www.phoenix.net/~melanie/thelogic.htm

A site dedicated to the study of the origin of words. "Are you curious about the etymology of a particular word?" asks the site author. If it's not in the site's copious archive, e-mail the site author and perhaps it will be added. *Paddy wagon, palooka, neck of the woods, New York minute, afghan, alimony, egregious, eleemosynary*—these are words and phrases whose origin and derivation you'll find here.

MLA-Style Citations of Electronic Sources

http://www.cas.usf.edu/english/walker/mla.html

How do you cite the Internet? According to Janice R. Walker of the Department of English at the University of South Florida, the *MLA Style Manual* "does not address the wealth of information now being made available to us (and to our students) via the Internet." Professor Walker fills that gap with means of citing websites, FTP sites, Telnets, MOOs, MUDs, IRC, Gophers, e-mail, and other sources. Endorsed by the Alliance for Computers and Writing.

Purdue University On-line Writing Lab

http://owl.trc.purdue.edu/introduction.html

Purdue students come to the lab to become better writers; you can, too. The index of handouts offers more than a hundred clear and useful articles that can focus your thinking and answer your questions about grammar and style. Topics include Invention/Planning; Editing/Proofreading; Style/Clarity/Coherence; Dealing with Writing Anxiety; and Other Issues/Topics. The essay "Overcoming Writers Block," for instance, offers some thoughtful ideas on getting going again: "If you don't want to spend time writing or don't understand the assignment . . . then resign yourself to the fact that you have to write the paper." I like that. Lots more tools and links. Delightful and highly useful.

Semiotics For Beginners

http://www.aber.ac.uk/~dgc/semiotic.html

Once I got drunk with an English professor who admitted the sorry truth: Semiotics is a bunch of nonsense that no one understands; it exists only to get grad students jobs at top universities. But if you don't think semiotics is meaningless drivel, you'll love this website, which walks you through paradigms and syntagms, denotation and connotation, intertextuality, and a bunch of other ways that certain self-styled intellectuals waste their lives. Semiotics has as much to do with real writing as Twinkies has to do with French pastry. I have spoken.

University of Victoria's Hypertext Writer's Guide

http://Webserver.maclab.comp.uvic.ca/writersguide/welcome.html

An introduction to the process of writing and the study of literature prepared by the University of Victoria's English Department. Includes essays on paragraphs, sentences, words, documentation, grammar, logic, and other subjects. I went to see what they had to say about words and found the subject broken down into subtopics: spelling; gender-inclusive language; and levels of usage, including formal, informal, and popular. For example, in formal terms, you're exhausted; in informal terms, you're tired; and in popular terms, you're bagged. That's fun.

The only trouble with using lots of hypertext is that there's no real flow—as soon as you've read a couple of paragraphs, you've got to start clicking to get to the next subject, and if your attention span is like mine, your mind can wander and so can your Web browser. But this is a very useful tool for people who want to learn more about the basics and the rules of writing.

Usage Experts Change Their Minds, Too

http://www.eei-alex.com/eye/usage.html

Anne H. Soukhanov, executive editor of *The American Heritage Dictionary of the English Language*, third edition, shows that usage changes over time. Here you'll find thoughts on words like *irregardless, arguably*, and *hopefully*. We review *The Editorial Eye*, a monthly newsletter on publication standards and practices, in Chapter 11, "Essays on Writing and Publishing."

Using Transformational Grammar as an Editing Tool

http://www.cramer.nmt.edu/~cpc/trangram.html

A highly technical paper on the ins and outs of transformational grammar, which suggests that an unconscious structure underlies every sentence a writer writes and offers ways of editing that make academic and technical writing a little less opaque. Anything that makes academic and technical writing easier to read is a good thing. This site is recommended for those poor souls charged with slogging through their colleagues' academic prose. If you're still bothered by things like when to use the passive voice, this one may be a little over your head. In truth, it was a little over mine, but that's okay.

Wired Style

http://www.hotwired.com/hardwired/wiredstyle/

Technical terms, buzzwords, and acronyms from A to Z defined by the editors, experts, and mavens at *Wired*, the "future-friendly" magazine. This techno-style guide started off as a single sheet of paper, grew, through active discussion as new terms surfaced, became a book (which you can order here) called *Wired Style: Principles of English Usage in the Digital Age*, published by HardWired, and continues to grow as a website. Check out their definitions, add your comments, visit a list of more traditional style guides, and contribute to version 2.0 of the Wired Style book.

The Word Detective

http://www.users.interport.net/~words1/index.html

The online version of "Words, Wit, and Wisdom," a newspaper column that began in 1953 and is currently syndicated across the world. You'll find previous columns, a "Word Detective Bookshop" featuring word and language books delivered right to your door, and witty ripostes to readers' questions about the derivations of words. Great fun. Want to know where "I'm stumped" comes from? Or the correct use of "momentarily"? You have two choices: Get a life, or visit this delightful and idiosyncratic website. Or both. Contains links to other word-loving places on the Web. You'll find more words about words in Appendix D, "Sites For Sore Eyes—Just For Fun."

WWW Resources for Rhetoric and Composition

http://www.ind.net/Internet/comp.html

Want to teach good English? I mean teach well English. Or teach good English well. Or both. This website offers Internet resources useful for instructors of writing and administrators of writing centers or writing programs at colleges and universities. With links to OWLs (Online Writing Labs) at schools across the country. You'll find 100 handouts at Purdue's OWL, including essays like "Comma vs. the Semicolon in Compound Sentences" and "Coping with Writing Anxiety." Hundreds more handouts from other OWLs, which you can borrow or modify to meet your students' needs. Also direction on getting started in HTML, online courses, and lots more. An excellent resource for writing teachers.

CHAPTER TWENTY-SEVEN

PUBLISHING YOUR WORK ONLINE

I like to be positive and find the good traits in people, places, and things. But I strongly recommend that new fiction writers do not publish their work on the sorts of sites listed in this section. As with Appendix B, "Internet Resources," these site descriptions are included because this book is about what's on the Internet for writers, and many readers will welcome the information. *However* . . .

Writers don't talk about being writers. They don't hang out in "literary cafes" and they don't "publish" online for free. They sit home and work and work and work at getting better. That's your job. I'm listing these sites because it's my job. I hope you're not the kind of writer who'll use them.

Dozens of sites on the Internet offer the works of heretofore unpublished writers. And all—not some, not most, but *all* of the fiction I've seen on the Internet is "writing-class level" fiction, the kind of work that gets a C in Creative Writing 101. That's nowhere near the level of publishable fiction. And online comments are offered—in good faith, mind you—by other writers who demonstrate equal ignorance of what good fiction is. If you stick around in these circles long enough, you'll start sounding like all the other unpublishable writers, eventually tire of the whole thing, and quit.

An example are the so-called literary cafes. Big-time, real-life authors don't hang around in cafes. They're too busy writing. Or they're out promoting, working at other jobs because they want to or because they have to, carrying on their family lives, or drinking heavily. But they're not squandering their precious writing time on unpublishable fiction.

Authorworks Fiction Database

http://oeonline.com/cybernews/author.html

A smallish collection of synopses of fiction, nonfiction, poetry, and other forms of writing, both published and unpublished. Although published authors might benefit from posting information about themselves in sites like this to draw folks to their own websites or publishers, unpublished authors should not rely on someone happening upon their work on the Net. If you want to get published, spend time making your work excellent and then find an agent or a publisher yourself by doing it the old-fashioned way: send them your work with an intelligent cover letter (see Chapter 1, "Agents"). If you've got limited time to write and promote your work, that remains the single best way to go.

Career Plan for Fiction Writers

http://www.Webcom.com/~victory/carrplan.html

A lot of what's here is rather obvious ("If you are writing novels, seek an agent" and "Submit new material via your agent"), but you may find some ideas that spur you forward. Be careful, however, with a lot of the well-meaning advice you get on the Internet. For example, you're advised here that if you post your writing to a newsgroup, it "could be interpreted by some editors as 'publishing' and would decrease the attractiveness of your submissions to them." Editors in the real world don't read newsgroups and don't care too much what gets published there. This sort of advice is actually detrimental to real writers.

Desktop Publishing Journal

RECOMMENDED

http://www.dtpjournal.com/

A gorgeous and resource-rich website for desktop publishers, offering information and advice on every aspect of the business. You'll find sections on art; technique; technology; project management; publishing news; vendor charts; links; a "toolbox" offering reviews of new software, Webware, books, and type; and an industry forum. Not surprisingly, the site is extremely well designed, and I recommend it highly for all do-it-yourself Gutenbergs.

Internet Inkslingers

http://www.uncg.edu/~agcowan/writers.html

Writers of novellas, as well as writers of short fiction, essays, and poetry, can post their work to this site, which is either very new, very small, or both. Just a handful of contributors at this time—but wait 'til people read about the site in the *Writer's Internet Sourcebook*. Then it'll be jammin'. You can also post comments about what you read here.

The Internet Writer's Guideline Listing

http://www-wane-leon.scri.fsu.edu/~jtillman/DEV/ZDMS/browse.cgi?all

A service of *In Vivo Magazine*, this site offers you information on how to offer your work (we never say submit!) to dozens, maybe several hundred, Internet publications. You'll find what the zines, journals, career guides, and other publications want; whether, how much, and when they pay; and how to and to whom you send your writing. You will find a lot of esoteric publications here, including things like "Burning Car"; "Happy Kitty"; "Kill Yourself"; and the "Las Vegas Computer Journal." Also "Romantic Interludes," "Poetry Harsh," and "Big Dreams." Hey, even Hemingway had to start somewhere.

InterNovel

http://www.primenet.com/novel

Professional writers (a fairly loose bunch of people) have written the openings to a bunch of different novels; you're invited to read the novels to date and offer your version of the next chapter. No fees. If your chapter is chosen, you'll get a royalty agreement, because they're seeking to have these babies published. Also poetry and short story contests. The first novel thus written, "Very Dead," is finished, available for your perusal, and out to various literary agents. You never know.

Online publishing sites

http://www.art.net.Links.litref.html

Here you'll find a long list of places where you can publish your poetry and fiction on the Internet. Links include the Amateur Canadian Poets' and Songwriters' Page, the Amateur Writers' Page, the Asian Poets Page, the Collective Memory Palace, Dialect, SciFaiku, StoryWeb, and several dozen other sites for those who would like to post their work on the Web. I've reviewed a number of similar places in this book; rather than repeat myself, you can visit this one site, check out the annotated links, and find the locations that match up most closely with your work and taste.

The Online Writery

http://www.missouri.edu/~wleric/writery.html

A project brought to you by the University of Missouri. This site offers forums for writers of fiction and poetry to share their work and solicit comments thereon. You can read the works, the comments, the comments about the comments, and the comments about the comments about the comments. You'll also find some links to other sites of interest to writers, most of which are either reviewed in this book or are duplicates of sites reviewed in this book. The real value of this site is in the ease with which you can post your work and get feedback from well-intentioned cyberwriters.

Pure Fiction

http://www.purefiction.com/contents.htm

A website for people who want to write bestsellers. The "Previews" section offers jacket copy and excerpts from new books, almost all of which are from Penguin. Competitions, interviews with authors, and yet another place to post unpublishable fiction. The section called the "Slush Pile"—don't they realize the irony of the title?—claims that "publishers and agents read these pages." My attitude is, oh, really? Which ones? You can add your own 5,000-word story or novel excerpt, but first you have to convince yourself that it isn't an exercise in futility. I dipped into a recent "Slush Pile" and I didn't see anything that might attract the attention of a professional.

Short Fiction Critiques

http://www.ntsource.com/~cgayle/

A place for short story writers (not novelists, not poets) to send their work. If the site author likes the stories, they're posted and available for readers' comments. Also a message board BBS for writers, online chat, an events board that lets you know about upcoming events in the chatroom, such as a "Young Writers' Forum—no specific topic."

My usual comment about this sort of site applies.

Writer's Gallery

http://www.onestep.com:80/writers/

Here's a place where heretofore unpublished writers can get their work before the public, or at least before that portion of the public that visits this site. Organized by genre (novel, short story, essay), the Writers Gallery gives writers a chance to get feedback and see their work, if not in print, at least out there somewhere. A public comment file, to which you may contribute, offers you a chance to see how these fledgling writers are being accepted. They tend to break down into "Enjoyed—Yes! Read more—Yes!" Or "No," depending on their mood and whim. Most of the reviews are favorable.

Writer's Publishing Toolkit

http://www.awa.com/nomad/toolkit.html

The Internet meets Dale Carnegie. In big, bold print this page announces "HOW YOU CAN JOIN THE PUBLISHING REVOLUTION!" A little weird, this website ("Overcome Print Publishing Constipation" reads one headline), but it certainly is enthusiastic about publishing "E-books," or electronic books. "However good your writing, getting published in the conventional way is becoming increasingly difficult and frustrating" (unless you've got a really good manuscript, in which case it's increasingly easy and delightful). But "YOU CAN DO IT!" the page promises. A wordy introduction to the process of self-publishing e-books, but the information is all definitely here.

CHAPTER TWENTY-EIGHT

ZINES

Sigh. What can I say about zines? A zine is a magazine, usually one published on the Internet, where no one gets paid. Their creators view them as labors of love, a means of getting their names and their work before a potentially large audience, and a way of connecting with the like-minded. Last night before I turned in, I was rereading my dog-eared copy of Gibbons' *Decline and Fall of Ancient Rome,* and I was reminded that just prior to the sacking of Rome, thousands and thousands of Romans began to publish their own periodicals, which they called *Zinebablia.* These Latin zines demonstrated just how far that once-proud society had tumbled. Cast your eyes on the title of today's zines and you'll see that the apocalypse is at hand. At any rate, if you're ready for a venture into poor taste and uninspired writing masquerading as the cutting edge, dive right in.

I've divided this section in two: First come lists of zines and information on what they are and how you can have your own; then come examples of what zines contain.

LISTS AND BACKGROUND

Email Zines Listing

http://propagandist.com/tkemzl/index.html

Here you'll find a list of 235 (at the time of my visit) zines and newsletters, with links to same. You can visit Cyber Turd, Fashion Stance, Meanderings, Dead Pig Digest, Phone Losers of America, Electronic Hollywood, fishwrap, Nerd Magazine, and a host of equally useful online publications.

E-Zine-List

RECOMMENDED

http://www.meer.net/~johnl/e-zine-list/

This list, updated monthly, contains more than 1,400 zines. You can search by keyword (such as alternative, art, media, movies, poetry, science fiction, software), by section of the alphabet, or you can just plain look at the text version of the list. A labor of love by John Labovitz. Each zine listed comes with hyperlinks to a website or an e-mail address; you get the basics about its raison d'être, frequency of publication, and one or more names of contact people on the editorial staff. Of course, with many zines, the editorial staff consists of one person. For instance, I clicked on Mainstreet Journal and learned that it's "A newspaper (in Dutch) from Amsterdam. The newspaper comes out monthly and is interactive. Participation is possible by sending in articles, reviews, or by joining the soap-story." They can be reached, incidentally, at *http://aaa-mainstreet.nl/journal/index.html*

How to Publish Your Own Zine

http://www.thetransom.com/chip/zines/index.html

Who can forget that classic short novel by Virginia Woolf, "A Zine of One's Own"? Certainly not your friends at *thetransom.com*. This excellent website offers you all the information you need in order to launch, edit, and promote your own zine. Essays on how to get started; technical matters; FAQs; listings of zines, news, views, and reviews—absolutely everything you could think of that's related to zines can be found quickly and easily in this extremely well-written, well-organized and absorbing website.

SELECTED ZINES

Belles Lettres

http://www.sunsite.unc.edu/lettres/html

Links to and brief descriptions of literary zines such as Oyster Boy, Currents, Cyberkind, and Verbiage; links also to other literary-minded sites, such as a memorial page for author Walker Percy and the Internet Poetry Archive.

Circuit Traces

http:/vanbc.wimsey.com/~chrish/Circuit_Traces/current.html

A technology-minded Internet magazine with fiction, poetry, reviews, and commentary offering a futurist/science-fiction bent. The site is highly decorated, but the quality of the writing is about the same as in other online places, which isn't saying much. Typical article title: "Cyberpunk as Literature: Shattered Reflections of a Post-Modern Future." Just because everybody else is abandoning literary standards once they get a modem doesn't mean I have to. Harrumph.

Cyanosis

http://www.system-zero.com/

A website dedicated to the free dissemination of information and points of view that do not enjoy the blessings of Your Federal Government. The word "cyanosis," as the website explains, means the purple or blue discoloration on the skin that occurs when not enough blood circulates; the metaphor is fairly clear. Alas, the quality of the writing is fairly weak. There's a lot of weird stuff in here, angry, paranoid, confused. For example: the short story "So You Want to Be a Cab Driver" begins this way: "Well, cab drivers are scumbags. Now I know you're a scumbag. Worse. You're a whore." You'll also find essays, interviews, and "poetics."

Often people think that they're being silenced for their ideas. Sometimes it's just because they didn't express themselves very well. But if you're looking for a place where anything goes, you'll find it here. And as Henry Kissinger said, "Even the paranoid have real enemies." Whatever.

Intertext

http://www.etext.org/Zines/Intertext/about.html

A friendly, bimonthly publication, each offering around four short stories to Netcruisers. Founded way back in the old days—that is, 1991. Readers and writers of mainstream fiction, horror, fantasy, sci fi, and humor are welcome to converge on this spot where all their desires can be fulfilled. Read what's there, subscribe, or offer your own stories. There is an archive of the approximately three dozen back issues along with a list of the stories the editors consider the best.

Pif

http://www.dimax.com/pif/

Pif is a literary zine publishing high-quality poetry, literary fiction, artwork, and movie criticism by new and emerging writers. This attractively designed zine, published from Honolulu, Hawaii, enjoys financial support from *Writers Digest* magazine and has a very professional air about it. You can click on the archive section and find previously published work arranged by category, you can read about the authors, and you can also e-mail the authors directly with your thoughts about their work.

Salon Magazine

http://www.salon1999.com/

A literary, political, and cultural Web journal with news, book reviews, short stories, and essays. Authors reviewed at the time of my visit were Naguib Mahfouz, Ralph Ellison, Shirley Jackson, and Mary Gaitskill. Interviews with authors—at my visit, Tobias Wolff. "Salon By Subject" lets you browse through lists of best books with excerpts from same previous author interviews, previous articles, and book reviews. How seriously do top writers take this site? Well, John Le Carré was interviewed here and then responded to e-mail questions from readers. "Table Talk," the Salon's e-mail forum, offers erudite conversation on books. A pretty impressive site, all in all.

Word

http://www.word.com/

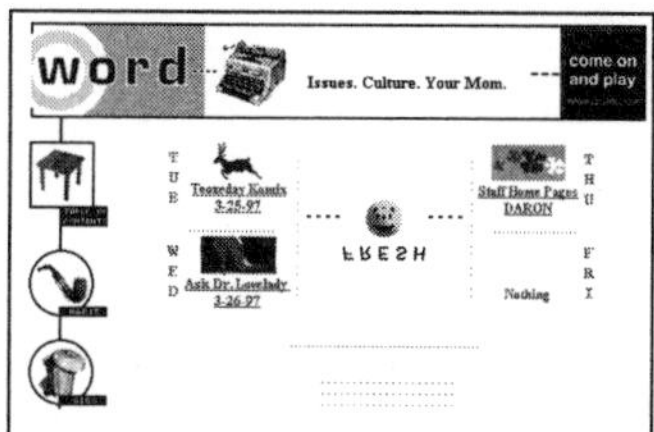

Politics, music, relationships, junk food, and sex dominate the discourse at this hip, lighthearted zine. Article titles at the time of my visit included the following: "If it weren't for Snickers, Patrick White would be dead by now. A real-life drama, straight outta Kurdistan." "John Albert Casey on the sickness, beauty, and plain stupidity of why people come together." Wake me when this whole zine thing is over.

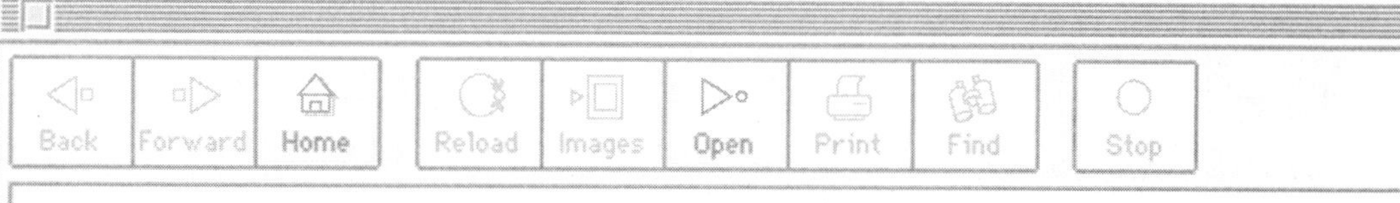

CHAPTER TWENTY-NINE

BLACK AND HISPANIC SITES

African-American, African, and Latin American journalists, poets, and novelists are described and honored at these websites, which feature reviews, essays, news, poetry, and university courses.

Barefoot Press—Poetry from South Africa

http://www.pix.za/barefoot.press/

Billed as "South Africa's first dedicated poetry website and home of free poetry." Poets whose work could be read at the site when I visited include Roy Blumenthal, Lionel Murcott, Rogers Ganhes, Alistair Dredge, and Elaine Rumboll. There are links to and addresses for South African poetry publications and Internet poetry sites around the world. You'll also find links to the journals of several writing workshops in South Africa, enabling you to find short stories and poetry by more South African writers. When they say "Barefoot," they aren't talking about being poor. The people behind this site apparently have a real thing for feet. The page lists links to foot-related and foot-fetish sites around the world, which significantly diminishes the seriousness with which you can take the poetry. Go figure.

The Black World Today

RECOMMENDED

http://www.tbwt.com/

This site describes itself as the leading source of information on the Internet about African Americans. You'll find news, opinion pieces, archives, sites to visit, and the "Ida B. Wells/Du Bois Network," a community of progressive African-American scholars, writers, and artists based in New York. An extremely useful site for anyone researching or writing about issues confronting Blacks in the United States and around the world. At the time of one of my visits, for example, there were feature articles on social, political, and military issues in the United States, the Caribbean, Africa, and Latin America. Highly recommended as well for elementary, junior high, and high school students and their teachers.

Chicana Literature

http://www.en.utexas.edu/~sheilac/readings.html

This University of Texas course, taught by Sheila Contreras, offers literature by Chicana women organized into a variety of topics, including "Las Familias"; "Bi-racial, Bi-lingual, Bi-cultural: Bifurcated Border Selves"; "El Otro Lado: Mexico and the Journey of Return"; and "Challenging Anglo-American (Middle-Class) Feminism." This will give you an excellent entree into the world of Chicana literature and also shows a fairly cutting-edge approach to integrating the Internet into the college classroom.

Isis: The Written Word

http://www.netdiva.com/written.html

A celebration of black women authors, playwrights, and poets. Here you'll find interviews, biographies, excerpts, articles, poems, essays, sound, links to authors' home pages, and even recipes. My favorite introduction: "If you don't get it after reading this [interview], you won't, ever." Lorraine Hansberry, Alice Walker, Audre Lorde, Connie Briscoe, Gwendolyn Brooks, Marian Wright Edelman, and Nikki Giovanni, among many other authors.

Quarterly Black Review of Books

http://www.bookwire.com/qbr/

African-American authors are the focus of this website, featuring reviews of current fiction and nonfiction titles, children's books, and poetry. Also includes the "QBR Guide to Black Classics," a "survival toolkit," and a listing of 11 essential African-American authors and their writings. The authors: W.E.B. duBois, Zora Neale Hurston, Langston Hughes, Richard Wright, John O. Killens, Gwendolyn Brooks, James Baldwin, Maya Angelou, Toni Morrison, Alice Walker, and Gloria Naylor. Also an author interview, at the time of my visit, with Terry McMillan.

NOTE

You will find more resources regarding black and Hispanic writing and news in Chapter 17, "Journalism Resources." Sites to visit include Africa Online, Hispanic Magazine, and Latino Media.

CHAPTER THIRTY

BOOKS ONLINE

You can push a few buttons, and any of 20,000 or more books can suddenly appear on your computer screen, or you may print them out. And it's all free. All of Shakespeare's works; thousands of classics; all sorts of wondrous and unusual out-of-print books. There you'll find all the books that you always meant to read (and all the ones you always meant to avoid).

We're not talking excerpts here. We're talking *entire texts.* Happy browsing.

Books on the Internet—A List of Links

http://www.lib.utexas.edu/Libs/PCL/Etext.html

If you want to see what books are available over the Internet—for free—start here. You'll find links to several dozen websites around the globe that offer entire texts of books. The "What's New" section offers a pretty strange agglomeration of books—religion texts, Jack London nonfiction, country studies of nations around the world side by side with the Bobbsey Twins. The "Online Books" from the University of Texas only has a handful of titles and nothing to write home about. Whoever puts all this stuff in some sort of order is going to rule the world. Fortunately, many of the other links are a little more sensibly arranged.

Books Online

http://www-cgi.cs.cmu.edu/cgi-bin/book/maketitlepage

Hundreds of books online—religious texts, literary classics, poems, science, history—arranged by title. You'll find *Civil Disobedience* by Thoreau, *The Civil War in France* by Karl Marx, and the *Code of Hammurabi* by, well, Hammurabi, for example. Now, this illustrates the strengths and weaknesses of the Web as repository of books: The benefit is that if you have a sudden urge for a particular book and you're lucky enough to find that it's on the list, you click once and there it is; click twice and you can print it out.

The weaknesses are that the odds, alas, are against your finding what you want quickly, although "quickly" is relative. It's a lot easier to spin around the Web than to get out to a library, where you risk that the book you want has already been checked out, misfiled, lost, or stolen. You also miss out on the "open stacks" experience, where you can serendipitously find not the book that brought you to the section but instead the book you really need. That's why sites like this really, for now, are just for fun. You can come across a neat title like *The Art of Kissing*, published in 1936, and you can read an interesting 1915 introduction to Hammurabi's code. But if you're looking for something specific, you'll want to turn to a search engine like Perseus at Tufts, which handles the classics, or Avalon at Yale, which publishes documents of American history and diplomacy. But drop in here nonetheless; you're certain to find something that will get your wheels turning.

RECOMMENDED

Classics of American Literature

http://xroads.virginia.edu/~HYPER/hypertex.html

Hats off to the University of Virginia for this wonderful and imaginative use of the Internet—here you will find the entire text, along with articles and sometimes photographs, of many classics of American and English literature. You'll find Stephen Crane's *The Red Badge of Courage*, Hector St. Jean de Crevecoeur's *Letters from an American Farmer*, Dickens, Joel Chandler Harris, Thomas Jefferson's *Notes on the State of Virginia* (how appropriate), Melville, Poe, Frederick Jackson Turner, and tons of Mark Twain . . . this could do a serious dent in the business of publishers who reprint classic texts. On the other hand, as Mark Twain wrote, "A classic is a book that everyone's heard of that nobody reads." How ironic that he should fall into that category. But these books are all waiting for you here . . . for free.

RECOMMENDED

The English Server

http://eng.hss.cmu.edu/

Read over 10,000 humanities texts at this cooperative website managed by students, faculty, and staff at Carnegie-Mellon University. Subject areas include art and architecture, drama, feminism, film and television, government, history, Marx and Lenin, and everything else you can think of that has a liberal arts bent. Read the texts, send new texts or comments to the editors, talk on the Telnet conference line, or join their mailing lists. If you can't find it here, it doesn't exist in academia. Period.

Fiction

http://english-www.hss.cmu.edu/fiction/

Novels and short stories arranged alphabetically by author. You'll find classics including the works of Jane Austen, the Brontë sisters, Bulfinch's *Mythology*, Willa Cather, G.K. Chesterton, Kate Chopin, John Cleland's *Fanny Hill*, George Eliot, Henry Fielding, Hardy, James, Kafka . . . you get the idea. I clicked on *Moby Dick* . . . and there it was, in all its extremely lengthy glory.

Great Books of Western Civilization

RECOMMENDED

http://www.ilinks.net/~lnoles/grtbks.html

From Mercer University comes a hyperlink version of the Great Books of Western Civilization, modeled after the famous course of study at St. John's College. The classics from Homer to Camus, with authors and dates, and here's the amazing part—you click on the name of almost any text in the canon, and boom, you've got that entire text right on your computer, for your reading, storing, or downloading pleasure. An astonishing use of the Internet. You will find reference resources for the Great Books Reader, Listservs and electronic discussions related to the Great Books, links to other Great Books programs, a timeline with links to appropriate literature and history websites, and a cafe for sharing your thoughts with other similarly inclined cybersurfers. Fantastic.

The Internet Public Library

http://www.ipl.org/reading/books/index.html

If you think this place isn't a real library, just try whispering or cracking your gum. One of the best reference areas on the entire Internet can be found here. You'll also find much for children and teens and a MOO. A MOO, incidentally, is a real-time experience where you can move around, speak, and hang out with other library visitors. You reach it by Telnet.

"The Reference Center" is what makes this site so valuable to authors. It offers books on education, arts and humanities, health and medical sciences, business and economics, computers and Internet, and other topics. There's a fairly stern looking reference librarian seated behind the desk that's labeled "Ask a Question," but I'm sure she's friendly once you get to know her. This is a phenomenal site, all kidding aside. If you click on **Arts & Humanities**, you get these options: "Fine Arts;" "History; Language and Linguistics;" "Literature;" "Philosophy;" and "Religion and Theology." Click on **Religion and Theology** and you'll find resources like a Biblical timeline; "Hitchcock's Bible Names Dictionary"; and something called "The Secular Web," a collection of materials related to atheism. You'll also find more than 3,700 actual full-length books are yours free, here. You can find them by author, title, or Dewey subject classification. This section of the Internet Public Library isn't nearly as strong as the reference part, simply because there are so few books. Thirty-seven hundred may sound like a lot of titles until you remember that a good college library contains half a million. I bopped over to the 700s—the arts—in the Dewey system and headed thence to the architecture subsection, which itself divides into "Architecture from ca. 300 to 1399" and "Buildings for Religious and Related Purposes." I tried the former and found one book about carpentry in medieval England; I tried the latter and found a Washington Irving book on Westminister Abbey. That was fun. Irving writes:

> "On one of those sober and rather melancholy days, in the latter part of Autumn, when the shadows of morning and evening almost mingle together, and throw a gloom over the decline of the year, I passed several hours in rambling about Westminster Abbey. There was something congenial to the season in the mournful magnificence of the old pile; and, as I passed its threshold, seemed like stepping back into the regions of antiquity, and losing myself among the shades of former ages."

So he wrote in 1819. This site illustrates the promise of the Internet and also the fact that, in many ways, the promise isn't yet quite fulfilled. I dove into a few other Dewey decimal locations here in the Internet Public Library and found no more than one or two entries per section, none of which looked like definitive works in those fields. This gives the Internet the feel of a musty, oddly stocked used book store in a hypermodern architectural building. There's interesting stuff in these online libraries, but unless you're looking for a specific, well-known, classic author or text, you're a thousand times better off wandering through the stacks of a real-live, book-filled university reference library.

NAP Reading Room

http://www.nap.edu/readingroom

I'm sorry, but the name of this reading room makes me laugh. Nap. Nonetheless, this looks like a good resource about science and government for technical writers or those fiction writers who want to introduce some factual material into their stories. You'll find books indexed by subjects like "Agricultural Science," "Biology," "Environmental Issues," "Mathematical Sciences and Statistics," and "Transportation." Unless you're Al Gore, you'll think "nap," too. The trouble is that the hyperlinks don't go anywhere. They're just empty. Maybe that'll change.

The Online Books Page

http://www.cs.cmu.edu/books.html

Here you can find 2,400 books. You can search through them by author, title, and subject, and you can also visit an astonishing site for a list of approximately 100 more archives of books and texts published online. All the sites are linked to this page and hail from all over the globe. For example, you can examine Russian literature on the Net via a website in Germany; "Project Runeberg," offering Scandinavian texts, from Sweden; the multilingual "Math Book Collection" from Cornell University; the "Literature and Medicine Database" from NYU; and "Italian Literature in HTML," from, not surprisingly, Italy. Also texts in Dutch, classical Greek, and Portuguese, among many other languages. The only tough part is taking a nap with your laptop balanced on your nose. I'm sure that enabling technology is forthcoming.

Project Gutenberg and Project Libellus

http://www.etext.org/books.html

All the books you were supposed to read in high school but didn't have come back to haunt you on the Internet. Project Gutenberg takes classics and little-known works by well-known authors, all of which works are no longer protected by copyright, and puts the entire texts of these books and stories on the Web. You'll find Jane Austen, Mark Twain, Joseph Conrad, Frederick Douglass, the King James Bible and the Book of Mormon, among many, many, many other texts. You'll also find texts related to science and mathematics, computer science, politics, and other nonfiction subjects. Well, maybe the politics books belong in fiction. A music section will offer classics that you can play via MIDI sound right over your computer. Project Libellus provides the same service for classical texts: Caesar, Catullus, Cicero, and Horace—all in the original Latin, naturally.

Shakespeare—The Complete Works

http://the-tech.mit.edu/Shakespeare/works.html

Shall I compare thee to a summer's download?

Thou art more fair and technical.

Rough winds do shake the darling baud of Macs

And hypertext hath all too short a date.

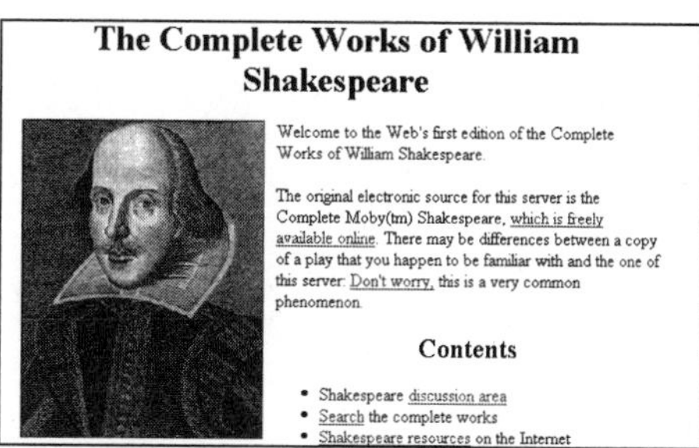

Every word Shakespeare wrote, with the exception of the early grocery lists, is available here, for free. Read the plays or search the texts for specific words or phrases. You'll also find a chronological listing of the plays, a discussion forum, familiar Shakespeare quotations from *Bartlett's,* and more. And, of course, all the sonnets. Most impressive.

CHAPTER THIRTY-ONE

GOVERNMENT INFORMATION

You can get census information, CIA dossiers on foreign countries, currency rates, medical facts, and the *Congressional Record*. And you can take a test-drive on the home page of the Information Superhighway. If it's happening in Washington, you can read about it here.

Bureau of National Affairs

http://www.bna.com

The largest independent, private publisher in Washington, "covering the interaction of business, labor, and government for more than 65 years." Mostly information about their books and subscription services, but you'll find online highlights from their *Electronic Information Policy and Law Report*, updated daily and available in full on Lotus Notes Newsstand.

CIA Publications and Handbooks

RECOMMENDED

http://www.odci.gov/cia/publications/pubs.html

To access this site, put $150,000 in unmarked bills in a brown paper bag, drive to Charlie's Diner at Fifth and Main any night at 11:00 P.M., and order the baked Alaska. When a man wearing a gray fedora . . . sorry, lost my head. The CIA publishes a vast amount of information about geography, politics, the environment, natural resources, economy, transportation, and communications for countries all over the globe. As a writer, you'll love this site because you'll get all kinds of wonderful background information for your stories. That's true whether you're a journalist, fiction writer, nonfiction writer, or even a poet.

You'll also find a fascinating history of intelligence operations in the American Revolution, ordering information for CIA maps and publications "released to the public" (darn, I was hoping to download some top secret stuff), information on the CIA itself, and a "virtual tour of the CIA." The only downside to visiting this site is that a dossier on you will be opened immediately. Just kidding. Sort of.

DefenseLINK

http://www.dtic.dla.mil/defenselink/

Greetings! The Department of Defense offers you information from each branch of the military. You'll start off with a quick, hyperlinked primer on the chain of command. That gives you links to the Secretary of

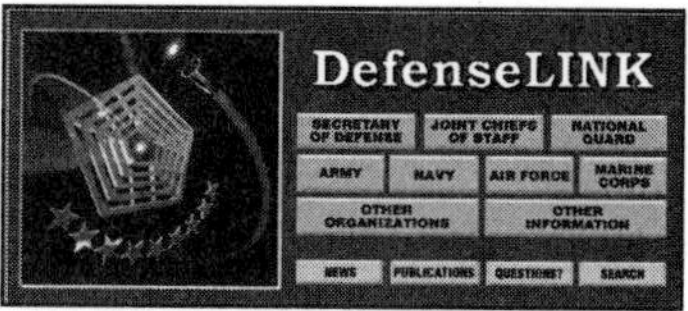

Defense, the Joint Chiefs of Staff, the Army, the Navy, the Air Force, and the Marine Corps, as well as links to subjects like education, history, countering terrorism, and protecting our forces. You'll then find official DOD news releases, photos, fact sheets, a search engine, and links to BosniaLINK and GulfLINK. Suppose they gave a website and nobody came? Not likely, with all the information available here.

Federal Reserve Bank of New York

http://www.ny.frb.org/pihome/mktrates/

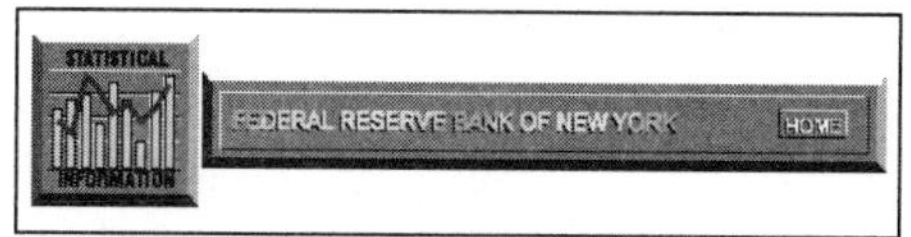

Here you'll find up-to-the-minute foreign exchange rates, commercial paper, historical rates, and other essential financial and monetary data. With a link to the Federal Reserve Bank of New York's home page—a cornucopia of financial information.

RECOMMENDED

The Federal Web Locator

http://www.law.vill.edu/fed-agency/fedwebloc.html

The "one stop shopping point for federal government information on the World Wide Web." Brought to you by the Villanova Center for Information Law and Policy, this well-organized website brings into easy reach all—and I mean *all*—the information that your federal government has placed on the Net. Legislative, judicial, and executive branches; independent agencies; quasi-official agencies; nongovernment federal-related sites—plus a special feature, "Getting the Most for Your Bribery Dollar, a Guide to the White House and Congress." Just kidding. An excellent approach to Washington.

Government Links

http://www.nwu.org/nwu/links/lnkgov.htm

A service of the National Writers Union. Here you'll find links to Congress, the White House, the Securities and Exchange Commission, the census, and other Washington information sources. Read the *Congressional Record*; track House and Senate bills; learn about SEC filings; Space Shuttle flights; and beaucoup more.

Library of Congress

http://lcweb.loc.gov/

Your tax dollars at work, and working hard: Many of the vast holdings of the Library of Congress are, or will soon be, available via this website. You can search the library holdings via Telnet. Another search engine allows you to tap into a phenomenal resource on American history. They're also working on digitizing millions of documents in the library and putting them on the Internet at this website; research will become millions of times easier. Current services include the following: Click on **Area Studies**, and you'll get a thorough overview of any of 71 countries around the globe. Go to the copyright page and learn everything that exists with regard to copyright law; you can even download copyright forms. (See Chapter 9, "Copyright," for more information.) And you can read *Civilization* and many other Library of Congress publications online and for free. Tons of legislative information. An excellent and most useful site.

Of related interest: Librarians' Resources

National Endowment for the Arts

http://arts.endow.gov/

Don't tell Jesse Helms, but the NEA also supports writing programs across the United States. Most of the website is dedicated to painting, sculpture, drama, and dance, but you'll also find background information on the current writing programs that the NEA funds. Includes an online bookstore and an archive of material about the arts, including writing, that's appeared on the website. With links to Culture Quest, the NEA's starting point for anyone interested in receiving funding for an arts program.

U.S. National Library of Medicine

http://www.nlm.nih.gov/databases/locator.htm

Here you can visit the U.S. National Library of Medicine and search their databases of book, journal, and information resource holdings. The NLM in Bethesda, Maryland, allows you to search on just about any topic in medicine or health. With a link to the Grateful Med Home Page (Who says medical researchers don't have a sense of humor?). I clicked into **HSTAT** and found a variety of databases, including NIH Clinical Studies, and a whole bunch of acronyms (AHCPR, ATIS, SAMHSA/CSAT) that mean something to the medically inclined. Extremely useful for writers who need information about any medical issue. Makes me think of Dana Carvey's line about George Bush's Health Plan for America—"Don't get sick!"

Of related interest: Medicine and Health

U.S. Government

http://www.tribnet.com/govt.htm

An excellent place if you're looking for any sort of government information. On one easy page, you'll find links to all U.S. government agencies, the White House, the CIA factbook, the House of Representatives, the Senate, the Department of Commerce, the IRS, the FBI, the United Nations, and more.

U.S. National Information Infrastructure Virtual Library

http://nii.nist.gov/

This is it: the actual, real-live home page of the U.S. Information Superhighway. Whoever wrote and designed this site should be flogged. Jargon, nonsense—a waste of time and taxpayer dollars. I read through the first few pages of this site and thought, too bad there's so much technical jargon.

Then, under "How Can I Participate and Contribute?" I found this: "Despite the bewildering technical jargon and media hype, every American has a role to play in the development of the National Information Infrastructure." My reaction: Do I have to? Can't I just write my novels in peace? This site is as vapid and pointless as any political speech—and maybe that's the idea. No links, no point, nothing but jargon. Your move.

This reminds me of the joke on Laugh-In: Dan Rowan asked Goldie Hawn if she was in favor of capital punishment. "Yes," she said seriously. "I think everyone in the Capitol should be punished."

CHAPTER THIRTY-TWO

LAW

The Internet is a godsend for anyone—attorney, journalist, novelist, or nonfiction writer—who needs to do legal research. You can find in the sites listed below vast amounts of important legal decisions, legal codes, articles, and rules. It's like having a massive, well-organized, and up-to-the-minute law library in your home. I happen to be an attorney and although I no longer practice law I know the value of the information in these sites. A legal library as well stocked as these sites would cost tens of thousands of dollars to equip and maintain.

Cornell Law School Legal Information Institute

http://www.law.cornell.edu/

Here you'll find recent decisions of the U.S. Supreme Court, the complete U.S. Code (federal laws); an e-mail address directory of faculty and staff at U.S. law schools; newsworthy decisions; articles on law and cyberspace; court rules (the Supreme Court's New Rules and the Federal Rules of Evidence), lawyers on the Internet, and links to other Internet law resources. This is an extremely useful site for many reasons. If you read about a newly decided Supreme Court case, you can find the decision in its entirety here. If you need to know exactly what federal law says about any topic, you'll find that law here. You can contact hundreds of professors and ask for their opinion on a piece you're writing; if you're courteous, I'm sure you'll get a prompt reply from most of them. This site is *not* for lawyers only. Dip in and be sure to visit the list of links to other law-related sites.

Counsel Quote

http://counsel.com/counselquote/

Astute attorneys understand the importance of marketing themselves and keeping their names in the public eye. This interesting site is a win-win situation: you get the information you need from legal experts in the field of your choice and the attorney gets to be quoted as an expert. If you need quotes from an attorney on any area of law, check this site in Chapter 17, "Journalism Resources."

The Law Library of Congress

http://lcweb2.loc.gov/glin/lawhome.html

"The Library of Congress," according to this home page, "began its existence in 1801 essentially as a collection of law books. But in 1832, Congress ordered the 2,011 law books of the Library of Congress separated from its general collection, and the Law Library of Congress was thereby established." It now has the world's largest collection of law books and legal resources from all countries. At this website you'll find the "Global Legal Information Network," providing an online database with information on the laws of more than 35 countries; the "Guide to Law Online," an annotated hypertext guide to legal sources worldwide; and information about making use of the Law Library reading rooms at the Library of Congress in Washington, D.C.

Legislative Library on the Internet

http://thomas.loc.gov/

"Thomas," named for famed 18th-century cyberhacker Thomas Jefferson, offers you your Congress online. The Congressional Record, bill summary and status, "Hot Bills" (presumably not the Clintons' legal fees), historical Congressional documents, and legislation databases await you here.

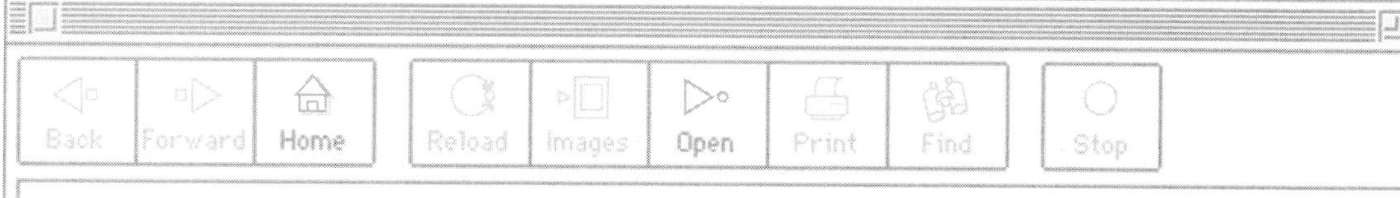

CHAPTER THIRTY-THREE

LIBRARIANS' RESOURCES

Librarians can use these sites to link with other libraries around the world, to answer specialized questions of adult and young adult readers, to keep up with news of library censorship, and to practice their shushing techniques.

Banned Books Online

RECOMMENDED

http://www.cs.cmu.edu/People/spok/banned-books.html

James Joyce's *Ulysses*; Aristophanes' *Lysistrata*; Shakespeare, Darwin, Mark Twain, even the Brothers Grimm, Judy Blume, and Anne Rice: all of these authors are or have been banned from public libraries somewhere in the United States. Read about censorship in America at this compelling website.

CARL—Magazine Search

http://www.carl.org/

This site lets you search through the full text of 17,000 periodicals by keyword and also lets you visit public and school libraries across the country, provided you've got access. Most individuals don't but most libraries do. Ask your librarian if you can access CARL either from the library or from your home or office. You'll be amazed: you can even ask it questions like "Who said 'Et tu, Brute?'" and you will receive an encyclopedia article about Julius Caesar, the full text of the Shakespeare play by that name, and magazine and newspaper articles. Definitely tell your librarian, "I want my CARL!"

The Data Research Homepage—With Arts Links

http://www.dra.com/

Data Research Associates, or DRA, provides computer services to libraries and other information providers. They have a gem of a website offering "Tricks of the Trade" (a "little shop of useful research tools"); links to "cool library sites"; lyrics of library-related songs; library trivia; quotes about the library world . . . do you think they're taking this library thing a little too far? Seriously, the useful research tools offer links to libraries specializing in art, dance, photography, digital material, law, maps, and much more.

Also available in French.

LibraryLand

http://ansernet.rcls.org/libland/

From the Ramapo Catskill Library comes a resource for librarians. Topics covered include shelving and display, security and materials flow control, reserves, inter-library loan resources, document delivery systems, online discussion groups, automation, electronic resources, audio-visual, and dozens of links to sites useful to librarians. Cutting-edge information for librarians preparing for the 21st century.

Libweb Links to Libraries Around the World

http://sunsite.berkeley.edu/Libweb/

A service of the Berkeley Public Library, this site offers links to libraries and their catalogs all over the world, arranged by country, state, or region. I clicked, just for the heck of it, on the Mustafa Inan Library at Istanbul Technical University. I was rewarded with information about the library, a connection to the university's home page, a history of the university, information about student life, and a faculty directory. A great way to find out about libraries and holdings from Cheyenne to China.

NlightN

http://www.nlightn.com

Type anything you can think of into this database and you'll get articles, books, database mentions . . . whatever. It's a service for libraries, but you can get a lot of information about various topics from your computer at home. Describes itself as "the Web's largest library of meaningful information." In order to read the database entries, you've either got to be a library or an individual (fee-paying) subscriber. Ask your librarian if you can use it for free at your library.

Young Adult Librarian's Help/Homepage

http://www.kcpl.lib.mo.us/ya/

Designed to gather resources on and off the Web to help librarians serving teens. Over 260 links, updated twice each month, and hosted by the Allen County Public Library, Fort Wayne, Indiana. Each link comes with a one-line capsule description. You'll find resources like "CRPC GirlTECH Home Page—Info about a program helping teachers help girls with technology"; "The Catholic Teen Page—Lots of links to teen and Catholic sites"; "The Student Center—Excellent page: well organized with plenty of links. MUST SEE."

CHAPTER THIRTY-FOUR

LISTS OF LINKS

The desire to put things in order is a basic human instinct, unless you're my five-year-old. (I don't really have a five-year-old but it just seemed like the appropriate thing to say.) But lots of people who come to the Internet say, "What a mess! Thank goodness *I'm* here to clean this place up! And they do. They find as many sites as they can that relate to a specific topic or theme. They put them in alphabetical order. They organize them into headings and subheadings. They add hyperlinks, so if you visit their list, all you have to do is click on the name of a website that looks good to you, and boom, you're transported there. (Or, more accurately, the content of the website is transported to you.) Sometimes they add annotations, descriptions, or ratings of the various sites. They are the neat freaks of the Internet. No one pays them; they get little glory.

But we are here to praise them. We love the people who pull together lists of links, because they make our writing lives so much easier. In this section you'll find lists of links of interest to all writers. Visit these list-bearing websites and you'll find the latest and the greatest; websites that were too particular or too slow relative to other similarly sized sites to merit a space in this book. If you bookmark the list of link sites you like, you can visit them from time to time and see what's new.

Book Links: The Overbooked Website

http://freenet.vcu.edu/education/literature/bklink.html

For cyber-do-it-yourselfers who want to see more of the Net than this or any other single book can provide. A massive list, actually a series of lists, of links to book-related resources, organized by idiosyncratic subject headings like "Genre Fiction: Mystery, Speculative Fiction, Romance," "Book Links Hot Picks: hot lit links and more," and "Major Book Sites/ authors/awards/children's and ya lit/book women/world lit."

Dive in, have fun, and if you stay there long, don't forget to write. Nice graphics, too.

Businesses, Governments, and Organizations

http://www.comlab.ox.ac.uk/archive/selection.html

A marvelously long list of links to everything imaginable. Companies like CBS, the Royal Bank of Scotland, Cadbury's, and Playboy; organizations like the Red Cross, UNESCO, and the Smithsonian Institution; and governments from the French Ministry of Culture to Vietnam and the Vatican. Also the Rolling Stones, Greenpeace, the International Monetary Fund, the World Bank, Xerox . . . I'm out of breath. You'll find a slightly British cast to the list, since it comes to you from Oxford. A great reference for writers and a better way to use your downtime than one more game of computer solitaire.

Clay Tablets—The Ancient Art of Writing

http://www.dingir.org/tablets/

A search engine offering more than 100 links to websites of interest to writers. Organized and searchable by topics like Contests, Online Forums, Organizations, genres, Publications, and Resources on and off the Net. Some of the categories have just a handful of links but you never know how these engines can take off. Worth a visit.

Miscellaneous Resources for Writers

http://www.aloha.com/~william/vpwfeat.com

Here are "64 Reasons to Never Leave Cyberspace." The split infinitive notwithstanding, this website offers you links to, well, 64 resources for writers, including the Chronicle of Higher Education, the National Creative Registry Online, Language Resources, and Talk Bizarre, billed as strange but interesting literature. Some are a bit too narrowcast-ish for this book so if you like the obscure and the odd, why not drop in here.

On Books

http://www.onzine.com/books.htm

When you visit this site, be sure to load the images. That's because these folks review about a dozen websites with one to four books; without the images, you can't see their reviews. Online annotations of the websites, which include a large number of sites for children's books. With a large number of unrated links to all manner of booklovers' sites as well.

Readers' and Writers' Resource Page

http://www.diane.com/readers/

Here you'll find books useful for writers, writers' tools (some super links), and a place to list your top ten favorite books. A smallish list but there's some good stuff here; and as with many such search engines maintained by individuals, there's always the possibility that things can change.

Science and Technology Bookmarks from Scientific American

http://www.sciam.com/bookmarks/editselect.html

Scientific American's editors have selected for your dining and dancing pleasure a few hundred science-and technology-related websites. Topic headings: Science News; Amateur Scientist; Archaeology and Paleontology; Astronomy and Astrophysics; Biology and Medicine; Earth and Environment; Chemistry; Materials; Mathematics; Museums; Government Institutions; and Searching the Web. I can't think of more definitive praise for a sci/tech website than the blessing of the editors of *Scientific American.* You can also recommend a cite for their consideration.

Of related interest: Science, Technology, and Computer Writing

The Writer's Corner

http://www.neosoft.com/~hgj/scraps.htm

This site refers to itself as "A cozy place for writers" where "there are still a few cartons of books to be unpacked, and the lighting's a bit dim, but feel free to call it home." The brainchild of Holly Jahangiri, this page offers a healthy list of links to writing-related websites including style guides, journalism, technical writing, young adult, stage and screen, and more; a writing room where you can post your fiction, essays, or poetry or offer comments to other writers; and links to websites dedicated to favorite authors and photographers.

The Zuzu's Petals Literary Resource **RECOMMENDED**

http://www.lehigh.net/zuzu/index.htm

A breathtaking website for writers and artists with links to over 2,000 websites searchable by topic or by keyword. The subjects dear to writers' hearts are these: "General Reference Tools," "References for Poets and Writers," "Writers' Conferences and Workshops," "References for Desktop Publishers," "Bookstores, Online Books, and Related Information," "Literary Magazines and E-Zines," and "Grant Information." The website's authors also produce *Zuzu's Literary Quarterly,* an e-zine featuring poetry and fiction that you can read here. This is one of the most amazing sites on the website; we highly recommend it for its thoroughness and ease of use.

CHAPTER THIRTY-FIVE

MEDICINE AND HEALTH

Any writer with an interest in medical issues will find a pharmacopoeia of information here. These sites will be of use to journalists, nonfiction writers, and fiction writers who want to sound extremely credible about anything concerning medicine and health. Every illness, every ache, every pain, every disease . . . and every cure, every approach to wellness, every drug, every doctor, every hospital, every medical library, every government report . . . are they all here? Just about. Even, as Woody Allen says, "the cure for which there is no known disease." You will be astonished and delighted at the amount of excellent medical information that awaits you in these brilliantly compiled sites.

Achoo—Online Healthcare Services

RECOMMENDED

http://www.achoo.com/

Dr. Download will see you now. The modest objective of this website, brought to you by MNI Systems Corporation, is "to catalog, index, describe, and evaluate the mountain of healthcare information on the Internet." How're they doing? Well, when I visited, they were already up to 7,700 links. You can type words into a search engine or you can search by the topics in the main directory, which are: "Human Life"; "Practice of Medicine"; "Business of Health"; and "What's New." I clicked on "Practice of Medicine" and found that it broke down into smaller topics: "Associations and Organizations"; "Education and Institutions"; "Government"; "Hospitals by Geographic Regions"; and "Medicine." A doctor friend of mine once told me, "We know that half of medical science is wrong. We just don't know which half." Well, you can do your evaluating if you start right here. They've also started an e-zine on medical issues; you can subscribe or offer them articles to publish.

AIDS and HIV Information

RECOMMENDED

http://thebody.com

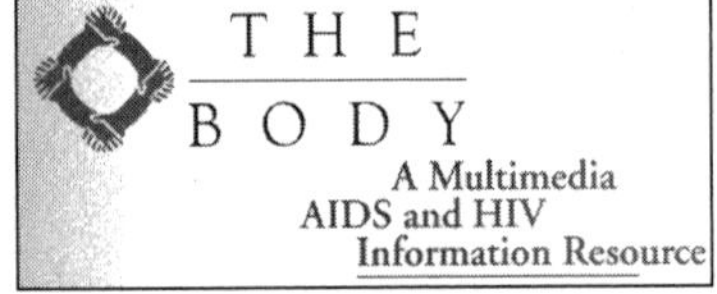

This extraordinarily thorough website covers every aspect of AIDS and HIV-related illness and treatment. You'll find Q&A sessions with experts on medicine, prevention, politics, sports, emotional support, and other topics; information on conferences and symposia; forums for "telling your story and connecting with others"; and a section on "AIDS—The Basics," with topics like "AIDS—What is it?," "Who Gets It?," "HIV Testing," and "On Learning You're HIV Positive"; and much more. This website has won awards from everyone you can think of; visit and you'll see why.

CDC Diseases, Health Risks, Prevention Guidelines and Strategies

http://www.cdc.gov/diseases/diseases.htm

The Centers for Disease Control in Atlanta have pulled together their resources on chronic, sexually transmitted, and other diseases; tuberculosis; injuries and violence; and behavioral and environmental health risk factors onto one easy-to-use Web page. With links to the CDC homepage. Click on "Sexually Transmitted Diseases," for instance, and you can download for free, "What We Have Learned, 1990–1995," a collection of research reports. You also get links to half a dozen related websites around the country. Let's be careful out there, okay?

Diseases and Disorders—an Alphabetical List

http://www.mic.ki.se/Diseases/alphalist.htm

My doctor says Mylanta, but medical writers and hypochondriacs will do backflips over this site, which provides hyperlinks to articles, websites, and gopher menus for every disease and condition from Acne Rosacea, Acne Vulgaris, and AIDS to Yellow Fever, Yersinia Enterocolitica Infection, and Zoonoses (both bacterial and viral).

Medical/Health Sciences Libraries on the Web

http://www.arcade.uiowa.edu/hardin-www/hslibs.html

Hyperlinks to several hundred medical and health libraries around the world, organized alphabetically by state or country. I visited Cedars-Sinai Medical Center's site here in Los Angeles and found a journal—holdings list searchable by title or subject and services including a search engine, a book catalog, and audio books. Chances are that some medical or health library somewhere on the planet can either answer your question or jump-start your imagination. From *Doctor Kildare* through *Coma* through *General Hospital* to *E.R.*, people are fascinated by stories about medicine. You can certainly get ideas for some stories by perusing the websites linked here.

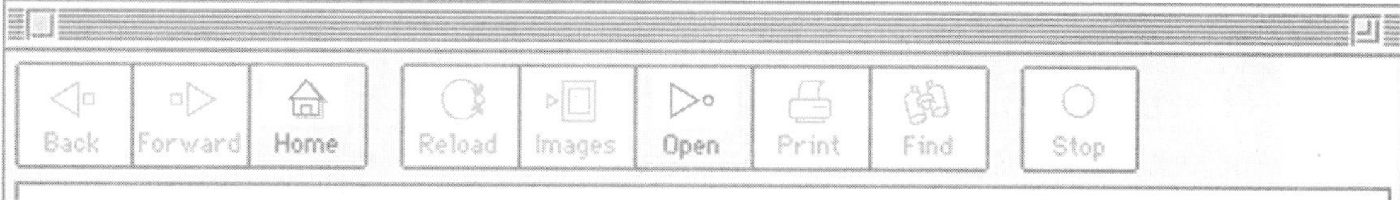

CHAPTER THIRTY-SIX

PRINT PERIODICALS—ONLINE EDITIONS

This section offers you the online editions of a number of publications of specific interest to writers. If you don't see a publication that you like to read online, check out the Electronic Newsstand at *http://www.enews.com* for a list of even more.

The *Atlantic Magazine* Online

http://www.theatlantic.com/

Articles and excerpts from the magazine "Devoted to Politics, Society, the Arts, and Culture since 1857—and a website devoted to the same since 1995." You can read articles from the current or previous issues; discuss same in "Post & Riposte," their interactive forum; send letters to the editor; or subscribe to TransAtlantic, their e-mail newsletter.

A year or two ago I met William Whitworth, the magazine's editor, in his office, and asked him how many short stories the magazine receives every month. "Twelve hundred," he replied. How many do you publish? "One," he said. "And how many of those twelve hundred do you read," I asked. "All of them," he said. And then the key question: "How much do you have to read before you know it's not publishable?"

The answer—and this is important: "One page." That's all. I believe him. This illustrates how important it is to get a story moving quickly. No one cares how good your fifth page is if they stopped reading halfway through page one. If you don't have conflict on your first page, don't bother sending it to the *Atlantic Magazine* or any other legitimate outlet for fiction. Just a casual reminder from your writer friend, Mike.

Boston Review

http://www-polisci.mit.edu/BostonReview/aboutBR.html

A journal of politics and literature, with essays and articles on subjects like the flat tax, abortion, and unions, as well as short stories and poems. You can read entire issues, enter the short story contest, or browse the "Democracy Reader," an electronic collection of political essays and debates on topics like "Race," "Class," "Gender," "International and Domestic Politics," and "Democratic Thought."

Mississippi Review

http://sushi.st.usm.edu/mrw/

The online version of one of the most highly regarded literary magazines in America. This zine has won just about every conceivable website award, including Magellan, Point, GNN Best of 95, and Blue Planet, presumably for the quality of its fiction. The writers are top drawer and have published in a wide variety of other literary magazines. The editor is noted author Frederick Barthelme, and you'll find eight works of fiction or poetry per monthly issue.

You are welcome to offer your own work for their consideration, and you can also enter their annual poetry and fiction competition. Details for entry available at the site. The fiction prize is $1,000, and the winning poet receives $500. That disparity reminds me of what poet Robert Graves told an NYU Business School audience. A student asked him why he wrote poetry when there was no money in it. "Ah," he replied. "But there is no poetry in money, either!"

Produced for the Web by the Center for Writers at the University of Southern Mississippi, which has published the biannual hardcopy version of the *Mississippi Review* since 1970.

The MoJo Wire—*Mother Jones* Magazine Online

http://www.mojones.com/

An alternative view of politics and society from the editors of *Mother Jones* magazine. At the time of my visit, you could find stories about the privatization of Social Security, the brewing Indonesia scandal at the White House, "money taken & favors returned by 12 of the most rotten eggs now sitting in Congress," and campaign finance laws. "Hellraiser Central" is how the site describes itself. A useful site for journalists and anyone who wants another point of view of your tax dollars at work.

Time Magazine Online

http://www.time.com

Time magazine's excellent online version offers you not just weekly peeks at the news but also an updated summary of each day's events. Click on **Time Daily** and you'll get several articles by *Time*'s staff on politics, social issues, and international stories, along with a search button that lets you find background information. You can also read articles from the current week's issue. The archives feature gives you the last six weeks' worth of articles from the U.S., as well as international editions.

The Economist

http://www.economist.com

The Economist is the best-written newsweekly in the world. No one competes with the depth and clarity of its economic and business news from around the globe. Its primary focus is the United Kingdom, but its coverage of U.S. politics and economic affairs is always fascinating. The newspaper (it calls itself a newspaper even though it looks suspiciously like a magazine) is edited for people with a college education. Currently, you can find excerpts from this week's issue at the website; shortly, you will be able to read the entire issue. There are links to other Economist Group publications. An added bonus: You can sign up for two free weekly e-mail versions of the publication, one focused on politics and the other on business. All you do is provide your e-mail address.

Back Forward Home Reload Images Open Print Find Stop

CHAPTER THIRTY-SEVEN

RESEARCH POWERHOUSES

This is one of my favorite sections in this book, because every one of these sites is jammed with up-to-the-minute information on one or a thousand topics of interest to you as a writer. The first section, Multitopic Resources, provides websites that alphabetize and organize literally thousands of websites, Gopher menus, and other great locations in cyberspace that will cut your research time in half. The second part lists phenomenal sites devoted to single topics—politics, the ancient world, space, myth, history, music, the Civil War, literature. Spend some time getting to know these wonders of the invisible world, so that the next time you need to do research, you'll know just where to turn.

MULTITOPIC RESOURCES

Argus Clearinghouse

RECOMMENDED

http://www.clearinghouse.net/

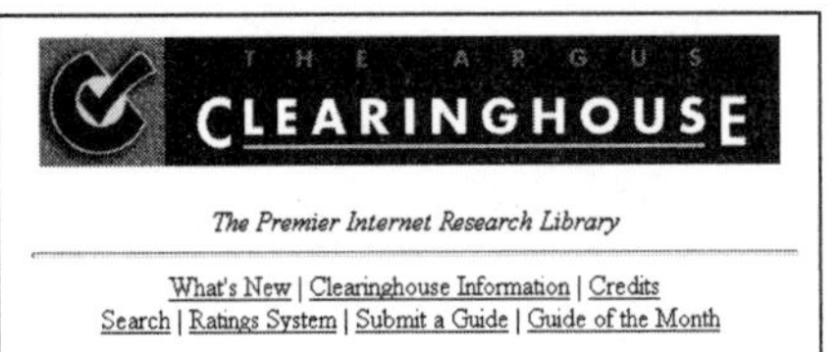

Bills itself as "The Premier Internet Research Library," and who am I to disagree? Librarians from the University of Michigan have visited, organized, and carefully rated what appears to be several thousand information reference sites on the Web. Here's how it works: You click on a main subject heading, and you're transported to a list of hundreds of websites in related fields. Click on a website that appeals to you and, before you get taken to the website, you'll get a multipart rating of the site. The Clearinghouse staff gives an overall rating of the website and then breaks it down into categories like "Resource Description," "Resource Evaluation," and "Guide Design." If you still think the site fits your needs, click on the word **hypertext** and you're linked. Main topics: "Arts & Entertainment," "Business & Employment," "Education," "Engineering & Technology," "Environment," "Government & Law," "Health & Medicine," "Humanities," "News & Publishing," "Regional Information," "Science," "Social Sciences & Social Issues." If it's out there, it's in here.

Gopher Jewels

RECOMMENDED

http://galaxy.einet.net/GJ/index.html

Bravo to David Riggins of the Texas Department of Commerce's Office of Advance Technology for this stupendous compilation of Gopher menus on an enormous variety of research topics. With a search engine and a help option. There must be a thousand gophers on this baby, which means that whatever your topic, chances are that you'll find a neatly organized list of essays, articles, documents, experts, histories, charts, graphs, maps, and periodicals devoted to that topic. Organized into more than 50 subject headings from "Agriculture and Forestry," AIDS and HIV information, and "Anthropology and Archeology" through "Federal Agency and Related Gopher Sites," "Genealogy," and "Geography," to "State Government," "Technical Reports," and "Travel Information." Breathtaking.

RECOMMENDED

Librarian's Guide to the Best Information on the Net

http://www.sau.edu/CWIS/Internet/Wild/index.htm

Why should librarians have all the fun? This is a spectacular site: worthy of a bookmark now and a visit later every time you start a new research project or simply want to learn some new neat stuff. Here you will find, or so the editors claim, the 1,500 best sites for information on the Internet. It's extremely well organized. You'll find 29 topics, from Art through "Chemistry" and "Geology," on to "Music," "Philosophy," and "Women's Studies"; click and find subtopics that take you to well-chosen Web pages concentrating on those fields.

But that's just the beginning: You'll also find a reference desk where you can get your questions answered along with links to other reference desks at other virtual libraries; jobhunting; "Surviving College"; news sites; disability resources, an electronic reading room featuring an astonishing array of political, judicial, and religious documents; picture sources—images from art, nature, medicine, and science—oh, my gosh, what are you waiting for? And "Sites for Librarians," where, presumably, librarians get to shush each other online.

Absolutely one of the most valuable resources a writer could hope for. Stop hanging out in dopey newsgroups. Come in here and learn something.

RECOMMENDED

Voice of the Shuttle

http://humanitas.ucsb.edu/

No researcher, academic, or student from high school to grad school will want to be without this marvelous and enormous archive of websites, online books, maps, links, articles, online libraries, online dictionaries and foreign-language thesauruses, biographies, chronologies, texts, photographs, museums, courses, journals, and other resources for dozens of fields of study. You'll find, *inter alia*, anthropology, archeology, architecture, classical studies, history, legal studies, literature, media studies, minority studies, and much, much more. It's extremely well organized and meticulously constructed. A fantastic site.

The WWW Virtual Library

RECOMMENDED

http://www.w3.org/pub/DataSources/bySubject/Overview.html

An astonishingly useful reference tool. Click on a topic from "Aboriginal Studies," "Aeronautics and Aeronautical Engineering," and "Aeronomy" to "Writers' Resources on the Web," "Yeasts," and "Zoos" and you'll be connected to extremely well-chosen links on the subject. I went to "Collecting" and found these categories: art and antiques, auctioneers, automotive, books and comics, trading cards, posters, and postcards, and seven more options. Vast and amazing.

SPECIFIC FIELDS

Alternative Politics—*Mother Jones* Online

http://www.mojones.com/

An alternative view of politics and society from the editors of *Mother Jones Magazine*. At the time of my visit, you could find stories about the privatization of Social Security, the brewing Indonesia scandal at the White House, "money taken & favors returned by 12 of the most rotten eggs now sitting in Congress," and campaign finance laws. "Hellraiser Central" is how the site describes itself. A useful site for journalists and for anyone who wants another point of view of your tax dollars at work.

American History and Politics: the Library of Congress

http://lcWeb.loc.gov/

Probably the most complete—and astonishing—resource on American history, on or off the Web. You'll find millions of documents related to American history. You can click on **Area Studies** and learn about 71 countries around the globe; you can also get full information about copyright services here. By all means visit the Government Information section of this book to find more about this website and to find many more sites where the government provides you with free information about countless topics.

Ancient World Web

http://atlantic.evsc.virginia.edu/julia/AncientWorld/html

Julia Hayden, a self-described "frustrated Etruscologist and Art Historian," has thoughtfully provided you with "a compendium of Internet sites discussing, spotlighting, or otherwise considering the Ancient World." Indexed by geography and subject. You'll also find an "Ancient World Web FAQ"; breaking news about archeological discoveries; a "What's New?" section telling you about recent additions to the website; and the search engines. Everything from "Ancient Documents" through "Cuisine and Cooking," "Gender and Sexuality," and "Mythology and Religion," all the way to "Theater and Music" and "Towns, Cities, and Other Places." A fine job; a wonderful sense of humor, too.

RECOMMENDED

The Avalon Project—Documents of American History

http://www.yale.edu/lawweb/avalon/avalon.htm

Just what you'd expect from Yale University: the Avalon Project, which provides the discerning cybersurfer with documents relevant to the fields of law, history, economics, politics, diplomacy, and government—with hyperlinks to supporting documents referred to in the various texts. Arranged by century (pre-18th, 18th, 19th, 20th) and by title.

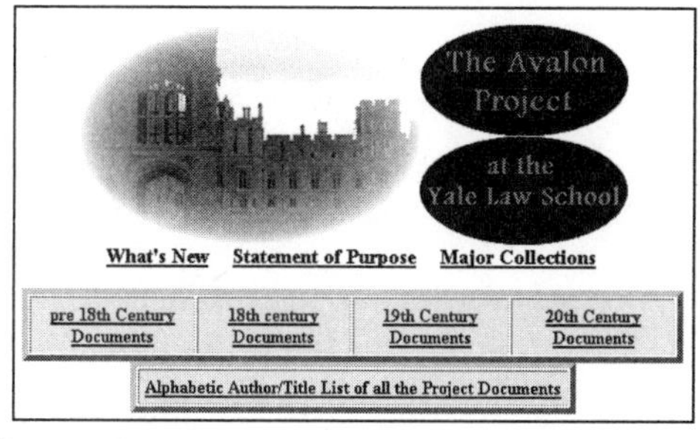

I clicked on the **18th Century** and found about 50 texts ranging from "The American Crisis" by Thomas Paine through "Washington's Farewell Address."

I clicked on the **Articles of Confederation of 1781**, and this precursor to the U.S. Constitution magically appeared on my computer. The "20th Century" offers the Balfour Declaration, the "Tonkin Gulf Incident of 1964" (one of the key moments in the early history of the Vietnam War), and the UN Charter. I clicked on the **U2 Incident** (that's when the Russians shot down a U.S. spy plane during the Eisenhower administration and has nothing to do with Bono getting drunk at the concert in Tampa). There I found six documents or statements related to that situation. An excellent resource for anyone interested in history.

Civil War Documents and Books

http://www.access.digex.net/~bdboyle/docs.html

An eclectic and highly personalized collection of links, texts, and references to (depending on your location) the Civil War or the War of Northern Aggression. You'll find "Christmas in the Confederate White House," Mark Twain's recollections of U.S. Grant, the examination of the body of John Wilkes Booth, the Constitution of the Confederacy, and much more. Civil War buffs and War of Northern Aggression buffs alike will agree that this is a well-stocked and fascinating site.

Classics Archive

http://classics.mit.edu/

An award-winning, searchable collection of almost 400 classical Greek and Roman texts in English translation, with commentary. You choose the author from a list of dozens of greats and, lickety-split (as Socrates used to say), the text pops up on your screen. I visited Homer and found the Samuel Butler translations of *The Odyssey* and *The Iliad.* It's also worth taking a moment to pause and reflect on the idea that our most ancient stories, plays, and poems—which three thousand years ago existed only in the mind of the author and a few hundred listeners—now live "out there" in cyberspace. An amazing juxtaposition of ancient literature and modern technology. Don't you wish Aeschylus or Aristophanes could have seen the Internet?

By the way, the Classics Trivia questions, frankly, are way too easy. This week's was "Which Greek author satirized Socrates, Euripides, and Cleon, among others?" Come on, everybody knows that's um, uh, can I have some extra time?

Encyclopedia Mythica

http://www.pantheon.org/mythica/

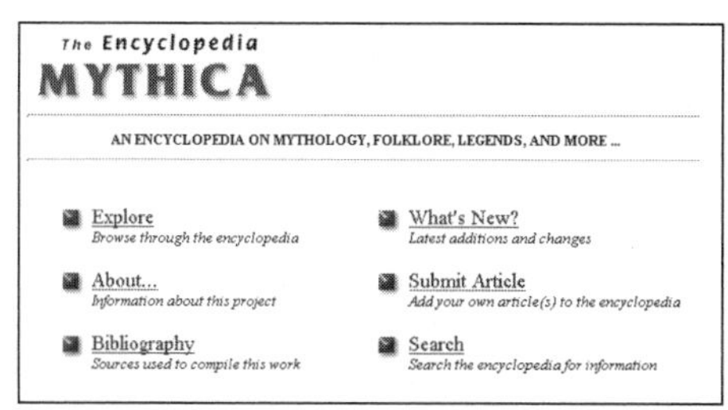

An award-winning online encyclopedia, beautifully organized, on mythology, folklore, magic, and more. With over 1,800 definitions of "gods, goddesses, supernatural beings and legendary creatures and monsters from all over the world." There is a link to the Encyclopedia Mystica, "for more on mysticism and the occult." Favored topics: unicorns, dragons, and Excalibur; gods and goddesses from Greek, Japanese, and Etruscan religions; places like Atlantis, Avalon, and Thule; and supernatural creatures like gnomes, leprechauns, and fairies. Because I'm a former Bostonian, I wanted to learn about leprechauns. I clicked on that term and learned that they are "very small sprites who sometimes live in farmhouses or wine cellars. They are known to aid humans and perform small labors for them. Sometimes they ask humans for supplies and furniture, for which in return they give objects which bring luck and fortune." I also learned that they make shoes for elves and organize wild feasts (during which time they are known as cluricauns, who often ride in the moonlight on the back of a dog or sheep).

There used to be a leprechaun who lived on top of the baskets at Boston Garden and used to help Celtics players by making good their errant shots, but he became a free agent, got a $67 million deal with an expansion team, checked into a cocaine rehab, and has never been heard of since.

A lovely website, and a wonderful place to visit with your children. Or, if you are a youthful cybersurfer, with your parents.

Historical Research Page

http://www.comet.chv.va.us/writersr/history.htm

Don't leave the 20th century without this baby bookmarked on your browser. Here you'll find links to Web pages concerned with history; the list is divided into basic categories of "Ancient History," "The Dark Ages/Vikings," "Medieval & Renaissance History," "Architecture & Art," "All things Celtic," "Costume & Clothing," "Music," "Asia & the Middle East," and "Assorted Historical Reference."

I had to laugh when I saw one site entitled "Byzantine Web Links," because the whole Web is, frankly, byzantine. But that's why I'm here, to make sense of it all for you.

A great reference site for historical novelists and history buffs.

Labor

http://www.igc.org/igc/labornet/

This site, which bills itself as "the only unionized website on the Internet," provides you with up-to-the-minute information on labor struggles worldwide and also offers links to labor organizations around the world. You'll also find a list of links to the kind of news services that do not normally get attention in the mainstream media. These links come to you from Washington, D.C., China, Russia, Africa, and Latin America, among other places. A search engine lets you type in a word or phrase and rapidly provides you with news articles and other references. I typed in "minimum wage" and got two dozen responses, offering news stories about minimum wage and employment issues from southern California to Korea and Vietnam. A most impressive site.

Literary Resources on the Net RECOMMENDED

http://www.english.upenn.edu/~jlynch/Lit/

An annotated listing of hundreds of links to every conceivable person, place, or thing in the history of literature. Search by keyword or choose a category like "Classical & Biblical," "Medieval," "Renaissance," "American," "Twentieth Century," "Theory," "Women's Literature and Feminism," "Victorian British," and many more. Each list has vast resources for you. The American section takes you to the "Jonathan Edwards Newsletter," "Poets in Person" (audio files), the "Walt Whitman Homepage," "Whales in Literature," and "The Fall of the House of Usher"—just a few examples.

The Victorian page gets you to Victorian Web at Brown, Victoria at Virginia Tech, Victorian Sensationalism Online from Alberta, Victorian Web Sites from Japan . . . what a wonderful resource. Thank you, Jack Lynch, from the University of Pennsylvania, for drawing all these resources together.

Music Archive

http://archive.uwp.edu/pub/music

In this archive you'll find a medley of music-related FAQs, articles, lyrics, and newsgroups, including "Folk Music Information," "Kurzweil K2000 Archives," MIDI software, "Classical Music Information," and tons more. I visited the "Lyrics" listing because I wanted to see whether copyrighted material had been posted. I wasn't the only one who was interested in that question. "Sorry," the page begins. "The Lyrics Page . . . is no longer available for public access. The University of Wisconsin was contacted by representatives of the music industry. On the advice of legal council, we have closed the archive[.]"

That's the dilemma. It's fun to have free access to lyrics and all kinds of other great stuff; the problem is compensation. Good for the music industry for protecting its songwriters and publishers. Some writers may disagree. But if they ever see a work of theirs, into which they put months or years of effort, suddenly available in cyberspace with no compensation to the author—they might, I daresay, change their tune.

RECOMMENDED

Music Resources

http://www.siba.fi/Kulttuuripalvelut/music.html

From the Sibelius Academy of Finland comes this monster list of Internet music links. Choose from the list of 18 main topics (church music, composing, computer music and MIDI, instruments, music magazines, orchestras, rock and pop) and you'll be offered dozens of links to music-related websites around the world. For example, the "Orchestras, etc." page offers links to a vast number of orchestras spanning the globe, as well as mailing lists for conductors, managers, and players, and websites of individual conductors like Esa-Pekka Salonen of the L.A. Philharmonic or groups like the Kronos Quartet. "Rock and Pop" has an unnervingly high proportion of Finnish links (Finland HOT 100, Finland Rave Info, Finnish Top 20 Single Album, Helsinki Club Info), but there's some useful non-Finnish stuff in there, too. Definitely a little stronger on the classical side. A great resource.

Politics Worldwide

http://www.klipsan.com/

This extraordinary website, brought to you by Klipsan Press, publishers of reference works on history and politics, gives you insight and background information into politics and elections around the globe. Is your main character running for mayor in Malta? Governor in Gambia? Get the facts that will make your reader sit up straight and say, "Wow, this person really knows his or her stuff!" This is a riveting website, even if you aren't touching on politics in your work. You've got to check it out.

Wisconsin Social Action Archives

http://www.wisc.edu/shs-archives/

The largest holdings in the nation on the subject of sociopolitical movements and issues. Socialism, communism, anarchism, Social Security and entitlements, welfare rights, civil liberties and free speech, civil rights, the New Left, and student activism. You can access the archives reading room to the computer catalog, or purchase guides to the collection. Not recommended for listeners devoted to Rush Limbaugh.

World Wide Internet Music Resources

RECOMMENDED

http://www.music.indiana.edu/music_resources

What do the Beatles, the Beastie Boys, George Balanchine, and the Blues Brothers have in common? Links to their websites, along with thousands of other musicians, groups, performers, choreographers, and composers at this wonderful resource. You can search alphabetically by individual musicians and popular groups, groups and ensembles (except popular), genres and types of music, journals and magazines, the commercial world of music, and much more. A vast and excellent compilation of music-related sites.

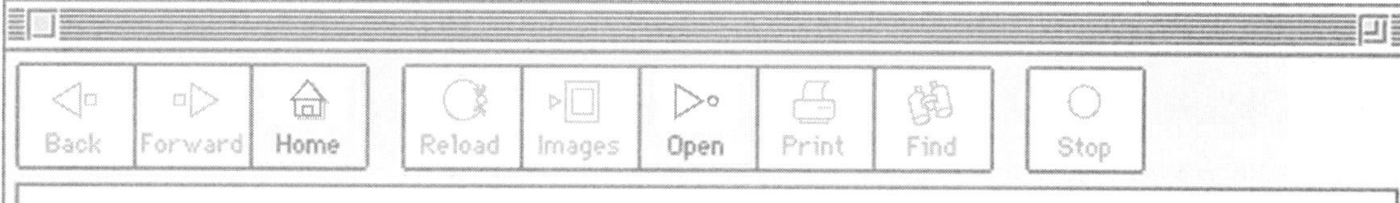

CHAPTER THIRTY-EIGHT

WOMEN WRITERS' RESOURCES

These websites focus on the achievements of women writers, past and present. You'll find a textbase of women's writing dating back to the Middle Ages; an alphabetical listing of women writers throughout the centuries; a literary agency that specializes in women writers; links to women's bookstores; and the publications of women authors of every race, century, and continent.

Bearlife

http://www.bearlife.com

A woman owned-and-operated literary agency that promises to "go to almost any lengths to help a woman establish her place in the literary community." Editing, proofreading, indexing, writing query letters, typing submissions, and putting them in the mail: Bearlife offers one-stop shopping for women writers who wish to turn the business of writing over to someone else. With lists of paying markets on the Web, tips on offering your work for sale, and an emphasis on poets. (This is one of the few agencies that actually seeks to represent poets.)

Brown University Women Writers Project

http://www.stg.brown.edu/projects/wwp/wwp_home.html

A textbase of women's writing in English before 1830. The lack of knowledge about pre-Victorian women's writing has "seriously distorted our view of the role of women in Western literary and cultural history." Currently, you can read, read about, or print more than 200 texts, among which are "The Mothers Legacie, to her unborne child," by Elizabeth Jocelin, published in 1622, and Anne Lok's 1560 "A Meditation of a Penitent Sinner." A fascinating collection of materials not easily available elsewhere. With links to related sites.

Celebration of Women Writers

RECOMMENDED

http://www.cs.cmu.edu/People/mmbt/women/writers.html

This site offers an alphabetical listing of women writers through the centuries, with links either to websites celebrating those authors, or, where copyright has expired, links to texts by those authors. You'll find, for example, familiar names like Maya Angelou and Emma Lazarus, and you'll also get the complete works of 17th-century Spanish author Sor Juana Ines de la Cruz. An excellent site.

Of related interest: Authors

Feminist Majority Foundation Online

http://www.feminist.org/

Feminist news from the worlds of politics, culture, and literature. An online store allows you to choose books and other items and purchase them via the website. The book titles include *Why and How Women Will Elect the Next President*, by former NOW president Eleanor Smeal; *Back Off: How to Confront and Stop Sexual Harassment and Harassers*, by Martha Langelan; and *A Private Matter: RU 486 and the Abortion Crisis*, by Lawrence Lader.

RECOMMENDED

Feminist Science Fiction, Fantasy and Utopia

http://www.uic.edu/~lauramd/sf/femsf.html

For readers—reviews, bibliographies by category, and recommended reading lists. For researchers—links to literary criticism, journals, zines, conferences, meetings, and a scholars' directory. For writers—publishers and venues for publication of feminist science fiction, books and short stories, related material, trivia, an index of women science fiction writers, quotes, a bulletin board, reading groups, fan clubs, and a search engine. A superb site.

Penguin's 500 Great Books by Women

http://www.penguin.com/usa/catalogs/readgroups/titles/bywomen.html

Five hundred recommended books (with annotations) by women—and ISBN numbers, for ease in ordering. Recommendations are arranged by these topics: "Choices"; "Conflicting Cultures"; "Families"; "Friendships and Interactions"; "Growing Up and Growing Old"; and more. The list comes from the Penguin book *500 Great Books by Women, A Reader's Guide*, by Erica Bauermeister, Jesse Larsen, and Holly Smith. A great use of the Internet—it provides useful information for free to readers, it helps sell Penguin books, and it promotes the book from which the list comes. Everybody wins.

Sapphisticate

http://www.saphhisticate.com/

This website teases, "For the dykescriminating reader," and was created to provide access to lesbian literary work by those uncomfortable with visiting gay/lesbian bookstores. Sapphisticate is a partner of Amazon.com, which fills all of the orders, protecting the privacy of the book buyer. You'll find featured selections; publishers; authors; reviews posted by visitors to the site; and an order form as well as detailed descriptions (with hyperlinks, if you want to order the book) of selections from the eighth annual Lambda Literary Award Winners.

Women's Bookshelf

http://www.womenbooks.com/

This online bookstore offers you information on the latest and the greatest in women's fiction, nonfiction, poetry, and more. You'll find descriptions of books; ordering information; a search engine allowing you to search by subject, title, or author; a list of new publications; and excerpts from books, allowing you to try before you buy. A most attractive and welcoming website.

Women's Book Reviews—A Cooperative Book Review

http://www.cybergrrl.com/review/

Six women reviewers (at this time) review fiction, poetry, and nonfiction by women authors from around the world. The purpose is to encourage women "to read women's books and to buy women's books at women's bookstores if they possibly can. "Loosely connected" with the Feminist Bookstore Index, reviewed in the "Booksellers Online" section of this book. When I visited, I found reviews of new titles by leading authors like Anne Tyler, Anna Quindlen, and Jane Hamilton and many lesser known writers. The reviews are just two paragraphs long and therefore of limited use; the site is more useful for learning about writers you don't normally get to read about elsewhere.

Of related interest: Review Sources

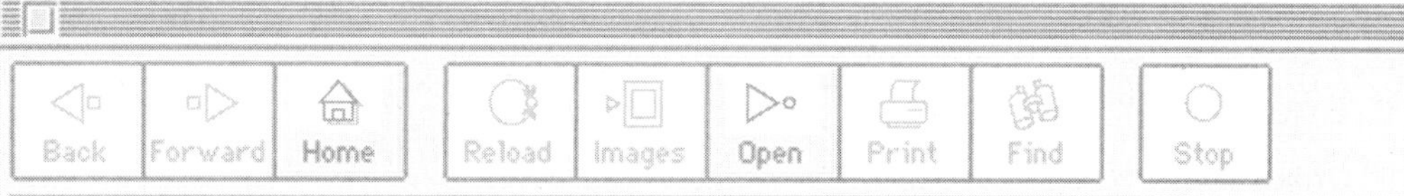

BOOKMARK ESSENTIALS

Most Web browsers offer you a feature called "bookmarking," which lets you simply click on the URL or name of any website, Gopher menu, or other Internet feature you like to add it to a list of Bookmarks or Favorite Places. Then, whenever you want to revisit that site, you simply open your Bookmark or Favorite Places file and click on that site name.

Below are 18 Internet sites that you might want to consider bookmarking. They include amazing services like free national and international telephone and e-mail directories; free access to all airline, hotel, and car rental reservation information; bestseller lists; an online *Roget's Thesaurus*; online dictionaries in every language; publishing industry news; and search engines that allow you to comb cyberspace in milliseconds to find exactly what you need. You may not feel like bookmarking every one of these sites, but each can save you time, stress, or money.

Airline, Hotel, and Rental Car Reservations

https://dpsl.travelocity.com:443/ezsabre.ctl

Turn your computer into a travel agency. Here you can get the same up-to-the-minute information on flights, fares, car rentals, and hotel rooms that your travel agent gets. It's all free. You can even buy tickets over the Net. Well worth knowing about. Easy to use. Highly recommended.

Altavista

http://www.altavista.digital.com

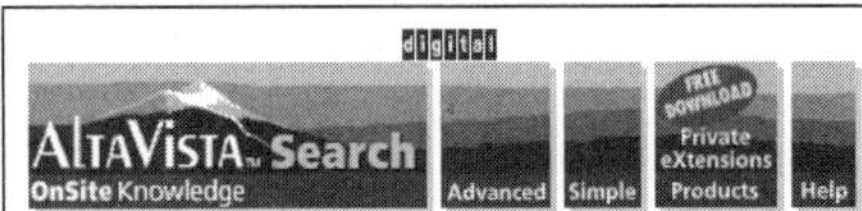

In our opinion, the quickest and best search engine around. Altavista basically searches everything on the Web and returns its results. If you need information about a subject, type the words that describe it into the search box and click **Search**. If you're looking for a specific name, title, or text string, enclose the words in quotes and you'll limit the number of results. Read their brief suggestions on formulating searches to eliminate a lot of wasted time and frustration. Our suggestion: put phrases in quotation marks, as in "chocolate pie" instead of chocolate pie. Come to think of it, some chocolate pie would be pretty good right now.

Bartlett's Familiar Quotations

http://www.columbia.edu/acis/bartleby/bartlett

Bookmark Bartlett's and never be at a loss for someone else's words. Yes, the entire *Bartlett's Familiar Quotations* is available to you via an exceptionally speedy search engine. I typed in **prune** and immediately learned that two authors, Alexander Pope and Charles Dickens, wrote quotable sentences including that word. You'll also find a clickable list of all the authors and sources quoted in Bartlett's, including Shakespeare (play by play) and the Bible. This comes to you courtesy of Columbia University's Bartleby Library.

Bestsellers—*Publishers Weekly*

http://www.bookwire.com/PW/bsl/bestseller-index.html

Here you'll find the week's bestseller lists from *Publishers Weekly*, the bible of the publishing industry. These top-15 lists include "Hardcover Fiction"; "Hardcover Nonfiction"; "Mass Market Paperback"; "Trade Paperback"; "Audio Fiction"; "Audio Nonfiction"; "Religion"; "Children's"; and "Computer." You can also search a bestseller database. Part of the massive BookWire site (see BookWire review below).

Bestsellers—*USA Today*

http://www.usatoday.com/life/enter/books/leb1.htm

The 150 top-selling books in the nation as compiled by the editors of *USA Today*. With links to articles about authors, books, and publishing from the pages of America's daily newspaper. Worth your time if you're wondering about what to read or what people are buying.

RECOMMENDED

BookWire

http://www.bookwire.com/

One-stop shopping for news about authors, books, booksellers, and libraries on and off the Web. First order of business: Note that the URL has a lowercase "w," whereas the name of the site has an uppercase "W." Now that we have that out of the way—you'll want to visit this marvelous site, which offers highlights from the current issue of *Publishers Weekly*, the bible of the publishing industry, and links to other book journals like the *Boston Book Review*, *New Asia Pacific Review*, and the *Quarterly Black Review of Books*. You'll also find links to more than 900 publishers, 500 booksellers (organized by type—antiquarian, children's, etc.), 500 libraries, and 1,000 other online resources. And you'll find information about authors on tour so that you can meet your favorites. This is a very easy way to find practically anything about the business of publishing.

E-mail "White Pages" Directory

http://www.four11.com/

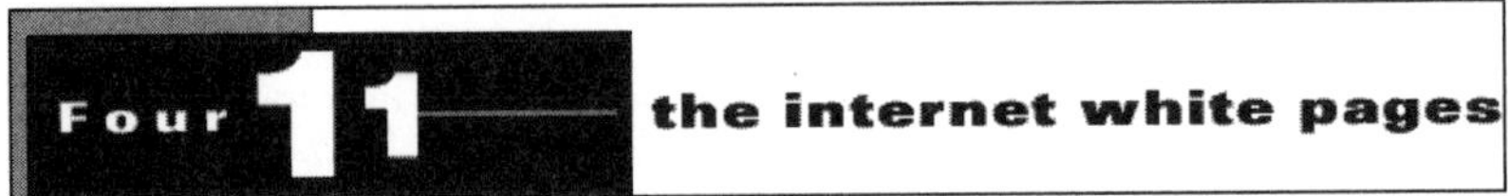

This free Internet white pages directory service lists over 8 million e-mail addresses. Search for friends, colleagues, businesses, or sources, or add your e-mail address here.

Excite

http://www.excite.com/

Excite seeks not just to list all the useful sites on the Web but to annotate and rate them as well. Some sections are more successful than others. You'll find weather; current stock quotes; stories from 300 leading newspapers and magazines; yellow pages; e-mail addresses; in short, a cornucopia of useful stuff—this part of the site is tremendous. But when you click on **Arts** and then on **Books** to find annotated and rated sites about books, you'll find that the selection is rather spotty. I've visited most of the sites they mention, and I don't agree with many of their ratings. I get the sense that their selector/evaluator is someone who knows plenty about websites but not so much about what a working writer needs. Excite might be pretty good in other fields, but I'm not enthralled with its current offerings for writers.

RECOMMENDED

Excite Citynet Guide to Cities and Towns

http://www.citynet.com

Okay, so you're working on a story that takes place in Texas, and you need some information for authentic local color. You can always jump on a plane and spend a week traveling the back roads of Deaf Smith County, but you may have a hard time justifying the time and expense to (1) your spouse; (2) your publisher; (3) your boss; and (4) the IRS. What's an author to do?

Why not drop in on Citynet, an awesome service from Excite Visit this Website and a bright, attractive map of the United States appears. Click on the state of your choice and get a list of cities and towns therein; click on the one you like and you'll get history, photos, architectural advice, business information, even a white and yellow pages directory. I dropped in on Calvert, Texas, which I learned is halfway between Houston and Waco on State Route 6. I learned that the gazebo in town is "no ordinary gazebo. It's unlike any gazebo in the world." Now, I don't have a scene yet in which the Calvert, Texas gazebo appears, but when I do, you know exactly where I'll look for the lowdown.

You can look up similar details about more than 150 countries around the world right here. I love this site—so rich with local color and detail, it's perfect for authors and for spies.

Links to Potential Story Data

http://nilesonline.com/data/links.html

You're one fact away from finishing that article, or you're casting about for a new story or novel to write. Check out the wonderful research website offered by Robert Niles, who arranges information for you by topic with clickable links. Fifteen topics at our visit, including agriculture; aviation; banks and businesses; crime; economy; education; energy; finding people; health; immigration; law; military; nonprofits; politics; and weather. I clicked on **Crime** and found links to the United Nations World Crime Survey; the FBI; the Bureau of Justice; and a list of links to "international and selected individual U.S., state, local, and campus crime statistics." An excellent resource.

Of related interest: Journalism Resources

My Virtual Reference Desk

RECOMMENDED

http://www.refdesk.com/

If I were trapped on a virtual desert island and could access only one Internet site (that isn't X-rated), I'd choose this one. A dozen weather Websites; stock market information; and an encyclopedia section that can only be described as "encyclopedic." In it you'll find 19 (at my visit) choices including "Atlas/Geography"(which takes you to 31 map websites, including ones for earthquakes and Russian commonwealths); history (over 100 websites linked, including the Origins of Humankind, Pompeii Forum Project, World War II Day by Day, and the Nixon Audio Archives); a phone book section with two dozen listings, including the French, U.S., and Swiss telephone directories; and "My Paper," which lists newspapers by country, state, and town. You can find seven newspapers in South Carolina, including the Spartanburg *Herald-Journal* and the Charleston *Upwith Herald.* Are you exhausted yet? I am. Bookmark this or make me wonder if you're really serious about this whole Internet thing.

National Yellow Pages

http://superpages.GTE.net

GTE offers names, addresses, and telephone numbers—along with key facts about businesses, schools, and services nationwide—drawn from over 5,000 yellow pages directories. This free service allows you to search by name, topic, location, or state. Also includes a Consumer's Guide, a car buying guide, and an e-mail address list.

Publishers Weekly

http://www.bookwire.com/pw/pw.html

The bible of the publishing industry. The single best way for new authors to learn about publishing is to get the last dozen *PWs*, read them all, and then go back and read another dozen *PWs* and then a dozen more. You'll get a sense of how books happen, what's going on in the publishing houses, and how the whole world works. *PWs* excellent website offers you book news; features; columns; book lists; a bestseller list database; and tons more. At the time of my visit, articles included overviews of the Latin American and African publishing scenes, lists of the all-time best-selling children's books (in hardcover and paperback), and a recap of the giant Frankfurt book fair. There is no longer any reason to let the publishing world be a mystery to you. Bookmark this site and visit it weekly.

RECOMMENDED

Reference Books

http://www.arts.cuhk.hk/Ref.html#dt

You could look it up: A complete set of reference books awaits you at this website: dictionaries; thesauruses (Is there a plural form of thesaurus? Thesauri? Thesaurae? Anyway, there are a bunch); and dictionaries in French, German, Chinese (the site <u>is</u> in Hong Kong; let's hope it survives unification with the Mainland), Japanese, Welsh, Esperanto, and ancient languages—Latin and ancient Greek. What an amazing concept: You can type a word into your computer and instantaneously connect with a computer in Hong Kong that will give you definitions, synonyms, translations, and even tell you—if the word is in ancient Greek—in what plays or writings the word appears. Actually, that Greek part comes to you via the astonishing Perseus Project from Tufts University in Medford, Massachusetts. But the whole thing is mind-boggling. You can also tune in here for updates on another astonishing Internet concept: the entire Oxford English Dictionary, soon to be available online.

Research-It

RECOMMENDED

http://www.iTools.com/research-it/research-it.html

Here you can look up a word in English and have it translated into French, Spanish, German, Japanese, or Italian—or vice versa. You'll also find pronunciation guides; a rhyming dictionary; an acronym dictionary; a biographical search engine; a Bible search engine; *Bartlett's Familiar Quotations*; maps; the AT&T toll-free 800 listing; currency exchange tables; stock quotes; and shipping and mailing companies.

Roget's Thesaurus

gopher://odie.niaid.nih.gov/77/.thesaurus/index

A searchable Gopher index—which simply means that you type in the word and hit **Enter**, and it gives you the synonyms. I tried "thorough," which is what I want this book to be for you, and it immediately gave me "completeness, greatness, melody, concord, restoration, and completion." I didn't quite catch the connection between "melody" and "thorough," so I clicked on "melody" and found a lovely phrase, "the hidden soul of harmony," the words of John Milton. I still don't get the connection but I like the hidden soul thing.

Savvy-Search

http://dns.uncor.edu/links/sitehelp/savvy.htm

Savvy-Search is to regular search engines what Altoids are to other mints. Savvy-Search calls itself a "parallel engine," which means that if you use it, you are simultaneously checking through a number of search engines (Yahoo!, Altavista, etc.) at the same time. Expert options allow you to tailor your request to the specific resources most likely to contain your answer.

Savvy-Search contains an annotated description of all the search engines you've heard of and plenty more you haven't. Worthwhile if you aren't getting what you want through traditional search engines. I wrote "traditional" even though the Web has only existed for a few years because I thought it would give a sense of history and place.

Switchboard

http://www.switchboard.com/

Telephone numbers, addresses, and e-mail addresses for more than 100 million individuals and businesses around the world. You can cut down seriously on your long distance telephone directory charges by bookmarking this site.

Telephone Directories Worldwide

http://www.contractjobs.com/tel/

Click on the country, and you'll find out what kind of telephone directory exists for that nation along with a comment. The Contractjobs folks called Infobed, the 4,000,000-listing Belgian telephone/fax directory "very nice." That's what you'll say when you realize that you suddenly have access to every phone book from Argentina to Yemen.

Telephone Numbers and Addresses—United States

http://www.zelacom.com/~hawthorn/database/director.htm

You'll find 90 million home telephone numbers and addresses and millions more business phone numbers and addresses available here—for free. Why buy CD-ROM phone directories—or even worse, call information for almost a buck a throw—when you can find just about anyone's number and address for free right here? An invaluable resource.

World Wide Web Worm

RECOMMENDED

http://wwww.cs.colorado.edu/wwww

Those are four w's, not three. Visit this site and find a search engine that lets you scan some three million websites by keyword or keywords . . . in moments. I typed in **toboggan** and, before I could lift my finger from the Enter button, I got two references to the Federation International de Bobsleigh et de Tobogganing at two different websites, which are, of course, linked. How cool is this? I thought I'd try a more literary reference, so I punched in "Vladimir Nabokov" and before I could say "Lo In The Morning," I found 15 references: addresses, criticism, courses, and biography. The downside is that you can pull up cites that have only tangential connections with your topic, or none at all, but this is still a mind-bending reference tool.

Yahoo! Authors

http://www.yahoo.com/

This massive search engine breaks down the literary world into 20 categories from "Authors" to "Writing"; hey, it's Yahoo!, so it's excellent. A good starting place if you can't find what you need in this book. As we go to press, you can go directly to *http://www.yahoo.com/Arts/Humanities/Literature*, but if their method of organizing changes, then look beneath the "Search" line on the Yahoo! home page for the section heading that seems to have the most to do with books.

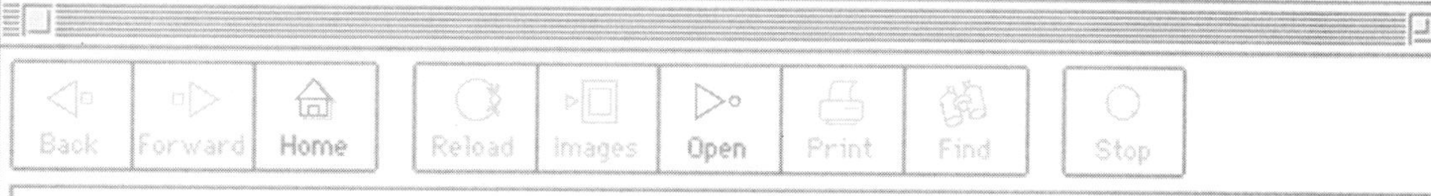

APPENDIX B

MAILING LISTS AND NEWSGROUPS

I include this stuff against my better judgment, unless you're using these things for marketing purposes.

First, definitions.

A *mailing list,* on the Internet, is a group of people with a common interest who sign up at a particular Internet location and then get e-mail from each other with regard to that common topic.

A *Usenet Newsgroup* is basically the same thing, except that the letters from members (called "postings") are kept at an online archive that you can visit at any time, whether you belong to that newsgroup or not.

You join a mailing list by sending an e-mail to a person, organization, or mail server in charge of that particular mailing list. (List subscriptions are sometimes automated so you're not actually writing to a person but to a kind of electronic robot.) Usually you'll be informed exactly what to write—generally something simple, like **SUBSCRIBE** in the subject line of an e-mail message. Be sure to keep the address and any instructions somewhere safe for the day when you choose to "Unsubscribe."

Instructions for reading newsgroups vary from software to software and service to service. Contact your service for their particular instructions or read their online help files.

The good thing about these Internet resources is that they bring you together with other people who like what you like, be it Jane Austen, science fiction, French existentialists, or screenwriting. The bad thing is that the comments about the various topics are rarely wise, and time spent with these sites is often time wasted.

A WORD TO THE CYBER WISE

There's something tantalizing about these Internet resources—it almost *feels* like writing. But I have visited many mailing lists, many writers' newsgroups, and chat rooms. And rarely have I found the conversation edifying.

Now, I don't believe in procrastination. I enjoy writing, so when I sit down at my computer, it's because I'm going to write. It's easy to call ourselves writers; it's harder to be disciplined enough to avoid distractions and get our work done.

I therefore list these sites with misgivings, because I know that some writers will use them as means of avoiding writing. I know that you are not that kind of person. The only real reason to use these sites is for marketing purposes. Take a look at the introduction to Chapter 13, "Promotion and Marketing," and you'll see what I mean.

Arts-Online

http://www.arts-online.com/writing

This project promises a bit more than it delivers, at least in the field of writing. The idea is commendable: to be a central place for hyperlinks to the homepages of *all* artists in *all* fields, including publishing. But currently only a handful of authors, one agent, one publisher, and one writers' group list in each of these categories. Still, it's an attractively designed site and one with great potential: It carries a "Top 5%" Website symbol, presumably for its more complete listings in other fields of artistic endeavor—dance, music, visual art, theater, and film.

Liszt

http://www.liszt.com/

A massive, searchable directory of more than 65,000 e-mail discussion groups, including at last count 167 involved with writing. A number of these are simply classrooms for specific university courses, but you'll find bunches of discussions of favorite authors, genres, and fields. My favorite: rec.arts.comics.creative, "encouraging good superhero-style writing."

Misc.Writing Newsgroup

http://www.scalar.com/mw/

As noted above, I'm not convinced that joining a newsgroup is the best use of a writer's time. Our job is to ponder life and then describe it; to hold, as it's been said, "a mirror and a candle" to society. People always have repaired to cafes to argue heatedly about the best way to write. Meanwhile, the writers were at home, writing.

Having said that, I can recommend this site not so much for the newsgroup, which offers the usual newsgroup sort of conversation, albeit focused ever so loosely on writing. The real reasons to visit this site are the other offerings here: You will find a well-written and accurate FAQ with the basics for those new to publishing. You'll also find an extensive annotated bibliography of books about writing, broken down by field—agents; copyright; grammar; inspiration; literary criticism; plays; romance novels; screenplays; and on and on.

Newsgroups

http://sunsite.unc.edu/ibic/IBIC-Newsgroups.html

A hypertext listing of 50+ newsgroups related to writing. Everything from alt.books.anne-rice; alt.books.stevenking; alt.fan.rumpole; alt.books.tom-clancy, and alt-fan.rush-limbaugh are linked here.

Newsgroups allow you to read postings, about various aspects of a topic and to voice your own opinions. You can meet other fans of a particular author or genre by clicking into the appropriate newsgroup.

Newsgroups on Writing

http://www.nova.edu/Inter-Links/cgi-bin/news.pl?writing

Newsgroups such as alt.fan.noam-chomsky, alt.prose., alt.startrek.writing-staff, alt.tv.x-files. Creative and computer and technical writing lists came up when I typed **writing** into this search engine for newsgroups. **Writing** brought in 18; **Fiction** 13; **Science fiction** 4; **Romance** 7 (but none of the 7 had to do with writing romance novels). Maybe you can find a newsgroup that's worthy of your time. As usual, my grumpy get-a-life attitude is, "Why not spend the same time searching one of the online book lists or get outside into the fresh air?" But if you like newsgroups on any subject, you're likely to find plenty here.

Writer's Block BBS

http://www.accsyst.com/writers/bbs.htm

This bulletin board service provides over 200 forums and five internationally conferenced networks, which is propellerhead-ese for "Come here and you can talk to a whole lot of other writers, online." Also games, movie reviews by users, and humor. If you've never used a BBS before, the kind folks at Writer's Block will be happy to walk you through the process. You can reach them via any standard telecommunications program, like Windows 95's version of Hilgraeve's HyperTerminal (information on how to do it is available at the website).

STILL MORE NEWSGROUPS

If you have other newsgroups that we should list in the next edition of this book, please let us know how we find them, how the sites helped you, and why others ought to visit as well. You can reach us at *writers@nostarch.com*

Be sure that you familiarize yourself with the style, content, and tone of any newsgroup before you post a comment of your own. Failure to do so practically invites longtime, crotchety members of that newsgroup to "flame" you—to criticize you publicly (that is, in the newsgroup) or privately (by filling your e-mail mailbox with nasty e-mail). Newsgroups consider themselves little communities with their own ways of doing things. As a courtesy to the current members, and as a wise move to protect yourself from their less courteous members, know what you're getting into before you post. The name of each newsgroup gives you a pretty good indication of what you'll find inside.

alt.anagrams
alt.arts.storytelling
alt.books.reviews
alt.books.purefiction
alt.books.technical
alt.censorship
alt.etext
alt.ezines
alt.fan.pooh
alt.humor.puns
alt.journalism
alt.journalism.criticism
alt.prose
alt.usage.english
alt.zines
k12.library
misc.books.technical
misc.writing
misc.writing.screenplays
rec.arts.books.
rec.arts.books.children
rec.arts.books.marketplace
rec.arts.books.reviews
rec.arts.poems
rec.arts.prose
rec.mag
rec.mag.fsfnet
sci.lang (scientific study of languages)
soc.libraries.talk
wpi.techwriting

APPENDIX C

CREATING A WEBSITE

The purpose of this chapter is to give you some links to sites that will teach you how to create your own Web page. Why would you create a Web page? It's an easy and inexpensive way for you to market yourself and your writing to millions of potential readers via the Internet.

Here's how it works: You design your own website or hire someone to do it for you. You can describe yourself and your books; you can provide excerpts, sample chapters, reviews, a picture of the cover; you can throw in a picture of yourself or anything else you can think of. Many authors provide free information about a topic of interest to themselves and their readers or provide links to other related websites. This builds goodwill and gives people a reason to come check you out.

If you add your e-mail address to your site, your readers can contact you directly—and you can build a mailing list to alert your fans about your next book.

The websites listed below give you information about how to learn Hypertext Markup Language, or HTML, the "markup language" that websites use.

Once you've created your own website, you then need to help people find it. Suggestions: of course, link up with the major search engines like Lycos and Yahoo! But you want to make it as easy as possible for people to come track you down. Remember that the major search engines often bury the site you want to find among hundreds or even thousands of sites that are useless for your purposes. How, then, do you make it easy for people to find your home page in cyberspace?

Here are some suggestions:

- Link your page to all the lists of authors mentioned in this book.
- Link your page to every list of links in the genre section related to your work.
- Then get imaginative: Go through all the chapters of this book, look at every single website, and ask yourself, "Is there any way that a reader who might be interested in me would check out this particular website?" If so, e-mail the site and ask to be added to their list of links.
- Finally, you can make it extremely easy for your readers to buy your books. All you have to do is visit the website of Amazon.com (you can read about them in Chapter 30, "Books Online") and become an "associate." Doing this is free, and it means that you can link your website to Amazon.com and people can buy your books from them. You get an 8% commission for every sale! Pretty neat, huh? (Of course, you could also sell your books directly from your site and rake in 100% of revenue.)

Chances are that your Internet provider already allows you to have a website for no additional charge beyond your current monthly access fee. This is certainly true for America Online, which also sponsors the extremely useful "Keyword: Personal Publisher" and other tools to help you design a decent Web page without knowing anything about HTML.

To begin your quest for a good Web page, start with the Eight Minute HTML Primer, the Introduction to HTML, or the Beginner's Guide, all listed below. The other sites are for folks who have been at it for a little while.

Eight Minute HTML Primer

http://web66.coled.umn.edu/Cookbook/HTML/MinutePrimer.html

What can you do in eight minutes? You can learn basic HTML coding with this clear and simple explanation. This page gives you a look at what an HTML-coded page looks like; in eight minutes, the authors promise, you'll be an expert, designing Web pages with the greatest of ease. Check it out.

RECOMMENDED

Introduction to HTML

http://www.cwru.edu/help/introHTML/toc.html

This site, the brainchild of Internet wizard Eric A. Meyer, gives you not only a full and thorough introduction to HTML but also the option of going on—via a hyperlink, of course—to the intermediate level. You'll find out what terms and concepts you need to know, and you'll learn about document tags, basic text structures, lists, anchors, images, and what you especially need to know if you're designing a website for an America Online account. This site makes sense even to non-propellerheads like your author. Highly recommended.

NCSA Beginner's Guide to HTML

http://www.ncsa.uiuc.edu/General/Internet/WWW/HTMLPrimer.html

If you want to learn about HTML, the language of Web pages, start here with this free (if it's for your personal use) primer from the National Center for Supercomputing Applications. You'll learn what an HTML document is; what all the terms mean; how to use markup tags, character formatting, and linking; and much more. Why not have a Web page of your own? Learn how here.

The Tao of HTML

http://www.taoh.com/index.htm

You can start with the Beginner's Essentials, but this site's special appeal is to those who are already knowledgeable: Tutorials. Style. Tips of the week. Specifications. How to validate your HTML and discover coding errors or missing HTML tags. Interactivity through CGI. If you want to take your Web page designing skills to the next level, this is your website.

Web Style Guide

http://info.med.yale.edu/caim/manual/index.html

This isn't an introduction to HTML authoring—you can find those nearby. Rather, it's a set of standards for how Web pages can be made maximally useful and attractive to the reader. Thanks are due to its author, Patrick J. Lynch, M.S., of the Yale Center for Advanced Instructional Media.

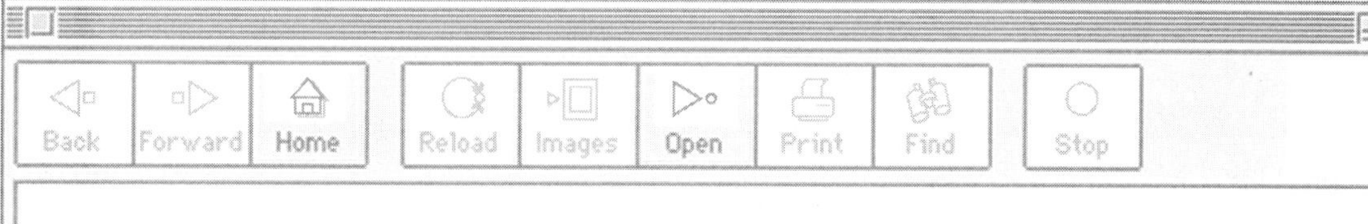

APPENDIX D

SITES FOR SORE EYES— JUST FOR FUN

Kick back and chill, as the young people say, with these delightful sites. Puns, anagrams, word games, quotes, *Calvin and Hobbes*, Monty Python, made-up words, comic books, and more await the writer who needs to unwind after a long day at the word processor. As Robert Benchley said, "I need to slip out of these wet clothes and into a dry martini." Slip into these sites and have fun.

A Word A Day

http://www.wordsmith.org/

This is the Web page for a mailing list that will send you a vocabulary word and its definition every day. Currently 56,000 people take part and will do very well on their SATs. You can subscribe by visiting the site; you can even send a gift subscription to anyone you know whose vocabulary could use a boost. The word the day I visited was *gainly*, meaning graceful or shapely. Great fun.

Acronyms Dictionary

gopher://info.mcc.ac.uk:70/00/miscellany/acronyms/.index/index

A dictionary of nearly 6,000 acronyms, compiled by V.I.P. Dave Sill. Interesting: It knew *snafu* (situation normal—all fouled up) but not *posh* (port outward, starboard home, the preferred location for staterooms on luxury liners). I tried a few things at random and learned that *SDF* stands for Secondary Distribution Frame and *TLB* means translation lookaside buffer. Now I can go write that novel. Seriously, this is just a fun use of the Net, and you might want to check it out PDQ (prior to downloading quintuplets).

American Literary Classics: A Chapter A Day

http://www.mindport.net/~arezis/

A novel idea: You can visit this site each day and read the latest chapter of an American classic like Louisa May Alcott's *Little Women*; *The Narrative of the Life of Frederick Douglass, an American Slave, Written by Himself*; or *The Red Badge of Courage*. And you can join the other readers in a discussion room.

I always tell my students that one of the key differences between publishable and unpublishable fiction is the way scenes and chapters begin. Unpublishable fiction scenes take a long, long time to get started. Good fiction establishes—in no more than two or three paragraphs—who's present, where we are, and how much time has passed since the last scene. Even if you're not up for reading a chapter a day of American classics, you can still get a lot out of this site simply by surfing over every so often and seeing how long the writers take to get their scenes started.

Remember that the much-maligned Ernest Hemingway, the author English professors love to hate (it's pure professional and sexual jealousy, by the way), broke American writing of its tedious, wordy traditions. So some of the 19th-century writers on this website, or anywhere else, might seem maddeningly prolix. But you, of course, would never do that.

A great idea and worth either an occasional or an extended visit.

American Slanguages

http://www.slanguage.com/

Choose any one of dozens of U.S. cities, click on it, and "talk like the locals"—that's the premise, and the promise, of this page. I went directly to Boston and found definitions of these words: *Seltz*—our basketball team. *Had*—opposite of soft. *Had Licka*—gets you drunk fast. *Buh Bluh*—water fountain. Okay, that was fun, but Boston accents are an easy target. I next clicked on Los Angeles, where (in my opinion) most natives speak English as though it were their second language. The definitions were great: *Gone Richter*—became angry. *Gummer*—senior citizen. *Tradin' Paint*—a car accident.

And so on. These are samples from *Slanguage Books* by Mike Ellis, who is making a delightful and successful career of gently poking fun at American regionalisms. You can order these books from the website.

Better Faster Be$t$eller$

http://www.c3f.com/bselcurr.html

Just for laughs: a parody, updated weekly, of the nonfiction bestseller list. Sample titles: *Al Franken Is from Mars, Deepak Chopra Is from Venus*, by William S. Burroughs; *It Takes a Big Fat Idiot and Other Slimeballs*, by Hillary Clinton with Al Franken; and *Anonymous Is a Big Fat Idiot and Other Observations*, by Anonymous with Norman Mailer and Faye Resnick. With "excerpts" from same. There's a lot of repetition in the humor in this website but it's still fun. Worth a visit if you're sick to death of Tetris and you need some other way to kill some time.

BritSpeak—English as a Second Language for Americans

http://pages.prodigy.com/NY/NYC/britspk/main.html

Highly entertaining and useful British-American and American-British dictionaries. You'll learn why one shouldn't compliment a British woman on her *pants,* along with definitions of *dodgy, fishmongers, knackered, spanner, treacle,* and hundreds of other words. Of use to anyone seeking to publish across the Atlantic; just good fun for the rest of us. Reminds me of Groucho Marx's favorite English town: Drooling on the Lapel.

Calvin and Hobbes Gallery

http://eos.kub.nl:2080/calvin_hobbes/

The website's author makes clear that he does not have copyright permission to reproduce the *Calvin and Hobbes* cartoons he publishes here. "However," he writes, "I feel the millions of Calvin & Hobbes fans all over the world should be able to see their favorites online." Well, by that logic, I should be able to drive his car or eat the food in his refrigerator, but who am I to cavil. A large selection of *Calvin and Hobbes* awaits you here.

How Far Is It?

http://www.indo.com/distance/

The fastest way to determine the distance between any two points on the globe is through this website. You provide city names, or ZIP codes, or latitude and longitude for practically any two places in the world, and Indo.com will calculate the distance before you can say "azimuth" or "Polaris." Well, actually it takes a few minutes, but you can add new precision to your work here.

Internet Anagram Server (I, Rearrangement Server)

http://lrdc5.pitt.edu/awad-cgibin/anagram

This website asks, "Did you know that *parliament* is an anagram of *partial men*? Or, *Clint Eastwood* an anagram of *Old West Action*?" This fascinating website lets you "discover the wisdom of anagrams." You enter a word or words and their computer, which clearly has way too much time on its hands, will instantly slice and dice your entry into dozens—even hundreds—of anagrams. I entered my name, Michael Levin, and got Claim Hen Evil, Clan Hive Lime, and Can I Level Him. No Starch Press, the publisher of this book, came out as Rash Scorn Pest, which is exactly right. Take that, William Pollock (Cola Milk Pillow)!

Jane Smiley: "Making Enemies: Your Bad Review"

http://www.bookwire.com/hmr/essays/smiley-review.html

A scathingly funny take on bad reviews by Pulitzer Prize–winning novelist Jane Smiley, author of *Moo* and *A Thousand Acres*. Published on the Web in *Hungry Mind Review*, the online version of the *Hungry Mind* bookstore's quarterly publication about books and bookselling.

If you want to take a break from your own work and have a good laugh, visit here. It's in the form of a letter from a reviewer to an aspiring author. "After I read your novel, I decided that the editor sent it to me because I live outside of New York and don't know you or anyone you know, and no one on the east coast would touch it with a fork."

JavaScript Word Games

http://www.netnet.net/users/jgales/game1.html

Have fun as you build your vocabulary: match words in one column with definitions in another column and the site tells you instantly if you're more like William F. Buckley or Alfred E. Neuman.

Jesse Sheidlower's Word of the Day

RECOMMENDED

http://www.randomhouse.com/jesse/

Ever come across a word that doesn't mean what you thought it did? Or just wonder what a "deipnosophist" is? Send your questions about words, grammar, or usage to jester@randomhouse.com and they'll be answered in this space.

Mr. Sheidlower is an editor in the Reference Division of Random House, where, according to the Random House website, he specializes in slang and new words. He currently writes a word column for *Esquire Magazine*. What's it to you, the busy cybersurfer? Well, Mr. Sheidlower graciously consents to accept your questions about the English language, and you can read his entertaining and educational responses here. A couple of hundred words are listed and explained here; not all of them can be reprinted in a wholesome family-type book like this.

Jonah Weiland's Comic Book Resources

http://envisionww.com/jonahw/comics/

Comic relief: You'll marvel at these comic book references, and you'll think Jonah Weiland is a superman for his incredible hulk of a website. Here you'll find sound files from television shows based on comic books; message boards; a chat room; links; comic book reviews; comics for sale; graphics from comic books; and information about the awards this site has garnered. Don't be a jughead; just drop on in.

Monty Python's Bookshop Sketch

ftp://ftp.borg.com/users/docrain/monty_python/BOOKSHOP

As transcribed from memory by a typically dotty Python fan. She has a phenomenal memory, because this is a long (and very funny) sketch. Leave the last word (BOOKSHOP) off the URL, and you'll find a long list of Python routines listed by words like *albatross, buttocks, cheese,* and *lumberj.sng*. If this isn't enough, visit the Monty Python website at *http://www.pythonline.com/*

Richard Lederer's Verbivore Page

http://www.tiac.net/users/rlederer/

The home page of Attila the Pun or Conan the Grammarian. More than a million copies of Richard Lederer's books are in print, and his column "Looking at Language" reaches more than a million readers across the United States. His website offers his entertaining and delightful columns on English and explains that there are far more than just three words in English that end in "g-r-y." Logophiles (word lovers) will also find a list of groups and periodicals devoted to "assuaging the appetite of the unrepentant verbivore," and can also check out Lederer's books, tapes, and speaking schedule. There are links to other language-related sites.

StreetSpeak

http://www.jayi.com/jayi/Fishnet/StreetSpeak/

According to this site, "A generation ago, people 'brown-nosed.' Now they 'suck up.' In the seventies, 'going fat' meant you had a serious weight problem. In the nineties, it means you have a serious snowboarding habit." Here you'll find definitions of neologisms, examples, and "Where Heard." My favorites: *to cybernate*: spending long hours holed up inside the house surfing the Internet. *Eddress*: e-mail address. *Alpha-chimping*: competing to be the dominant male. I don't know how authoritative this site can truly be, because most of the words listed were coined by the author or his friends: "My friends and I made it up," "My friend Jen and I made it up while we were in France." Other sources include college roommates, camp, and "my uncle playing Scrabble." I wouldn't play Scrabble with anyone in the website author's entire family, at least not without a nearby dictionary with which to thump them over the head if they try to play *dawg*, *flava*, or *reesty*. A very entertaining site. My spell check will have conniptions, but that's the price you pay.

The Pun Page

http://www.erols.com/jwater

What do prisoners use to call each other? Answer: cell phones. Who said "Let them eat assorted meat by-products"? Marie Spam-toinette. If you enjoy this sort of verbal humor, you'll enjoy this page, which purports to present a pun a day. The site author, a law student, says that he gets behind on his puns during finals time, but you'll find links to other pun-happy sites. Just remember, never make puns on your first date. With links to a page devoted to lawyer jokes.

Today in History

http://www.scopesys.com/anyday/

This fun site lets you look up any day of the year and find out who was born, who died, and what historical events happened on that day. I learned that I share my birthday, August 8, with Dustin Hoffman and Robin Quivers, and that the Battle of Britain began on that date in 1940. Just for fun, but you never know how a fact you turn up can turn into a story idea. (There I go, being serious again.) This site is a lot of fun, and that's reason enough for you to drop in.

Word Puzzler's Corner

http://www.niagara.com/~wrdpuzlr/default.html

Dozens and dozens of crossword and "word fits" puzzles await you here; with links to other word puzzle websites.

Writers Free Reference

http://www.writers-free-reference.com/

Here you'll find newspapers from all over the globe, births, deaths, and events on every date of the year, and other delightful and idiosyncratic links. My favorite part of this website is the "Good Quotes by Famous People": Here I found A. J. Liebling saying "I can write better than anyone who can write faster, and I can write faster than anyone who can write better." He also said "The way to write is well."

INDEX

C

D

E

F

G

H

I

L

M

N

O

Q

R

S

T

Y

Z

About the Author

Michael Levin is the author of nine books, including *The Guide to the Jewish Internet* by No Starch Press. He has published three novels with Simon & Schuster and two novels with Putnam/Berkley, and has written for a wide variety of media including the *New York Times*, the *Los Angeles Times*, the *Boston Globe*, the *Jerusalem Post*, and CBS News. He teaches in the writing programs at UCLA and New York University and is a council member of the Authors Guild. He is a graduate of Amherst College and Columbia Law School and is a member of the bar of the Commonwealth of Massachusetts.

I Lost My Baby, My Pickup, and My Guitar on the Information Highway

A Humorous Trip Down the Highways, Byways, and Backroads of Information Technology

by JUDY HEIM

"I Lost My Baby *is a funny book whether you work in the industry or are barely computer-literate. Get it."* —COMPUTER CURRENTS

If you're desperate for a laugh at the expense of your PC, the wait is over. Here's your chance to poke fun at your machine and at the people who created it. *I Lost My Baby, My Pickup, and My Guitar on the Information Highway* is an irreverent book by *PC World* columnist and computer-curmudgeon Judy Heim. It's salvation for people whose desks are heaped with blinking boxes and who dream of murdering their computer. Designed to be read either in snippets or in one sitting, it's filled with offbeat tips and vignettes, ranging from how to keep from weeping over your PC, to details of finding love in cyberspace, and finally to the universal truth: "Computers are faster than people, but only when people are brain-dead."

JUDY HEIM has also written *The Needlecrafter's Computer Companion* and *Internet for Cats*, and is the co-author of *The Quilter's Computer Companion* (all from No Starch Press).

128 pp., $9.95 (Canada $13.95)
ISBN 1-886411-00-X

The No B.S. Guide to Windows 95

by SCOTT SPANBAUER

"*. . . a no-nonsense guide for people who already know how to use a mouse and double-click on an icon.*"—NEW YORK TIMES

If you can figure out how to launch programs from Windows 95, this book is for you. You'll find clear, pithy answers to questions like: How do I unclutter my desktop and manage long file names? How do I use Exchange and Microsoft Fax? What should I do with config.sys and autoexec.bat? How do I manage memory under Windows 95? How do I connect my laptop and desktop computers and synchronize files? How can I tweak the Registry safely? Where can I get free updates and add-ons, and which ones are worth downloading? All without the B.S.

SCOTT SPANBAUER is a *PC World* contributing editor, the author of *PC World's* "Help Line Q&A" column, and a contributor to *The PC Bible* (Peachpit Press). Visit Scott at *http://www.indra.com/~scott.*

190 pp., $19.00 (Canada $26.95)
ISBN 1-886411-05-0

Dr. Bob's Painless Guide to the Internet

& Amazing Things You Can Do with E-mail

by BOB "DR. BOB" RANKIN

"... simple, hassle-free net surfing with a minimum of reading ... written by Bob Rankin, the driver of the widely acclaimed Internet TourBus."—NETGUIDE MAGAZINE

Whether you connect to the Internet through e-mail alone or the latest Netscape beta, *Dr. Bob's Painless Guide to the Internet* will show you how to use every Internet tool—not just the Web. You'll learn how to send and receive e-mail, find the cool and useful websites, search for and download the files you want, read newsgroups and subscribe to mailing lists, chat online, and more. Includes a glossary of terms and the "Internet Mini-Yellow Pages," with lots of useful Internet resources for you to enjoy right away.

BOB RANKIN is the author of *Dr. Bob's Painless Guide To The Internet* and *The No B.S. Guide to Linux* (both from No Starch Press). Bob is a columnist for *Boardwatch Magazine* and a contributor to several computer publications. He is also well known for his "Accessing The Internet By E-Mail" FAQ (read by hundreds of thousands of people around the world and translated into more than fifteen languages) and is the publisher of the *Internet TourBus* e-zine, an e-mail "tour" of fun and interesting things on the Net.

152 pp., $12.95 (Canada $18.25)
ISBN 1-886411-09-3

Distributed to the book trade by Publishers Group West

If you can't find No Starch Press titles in your local bookstore, here's how to order directly from us (we accept MasterCard, Visa, and checks or money orders—sorry, no CODs):

Phone:
1 (800) 420-7240 or
(415) 284-9900
Monday through Friday,
8 a.m. to 5 p.m. (PST)

Fax:
(415) 284-9955
24 hours a day,
7 days a week

E-mail:
sales@nostarch.com

Web:
http://www.nostarch.com

Mail:
No Starch Press, Dept. LX97
401 China Basin St., Ste. 108
San Francisco, CA 94107-2192
USA